THE TITANIC
★ EXPERIENCE ★

BEAU RIFFENBURGH

CARLTON
BOOKS

CONTENTS

INTRODUCTION

Perhaps no ship in history has engendered such continued worldwide fascination as the White Star Line's ill-fated *Titanic*. The largest man-made object ever to have been moved when she was launched at Harland & Wolff's Belfast shipyard in May 1911, within the next 10 months she had also become the most luxuriously opulent ship ever to grace the waves. Everything about her was stunningly impressive, from her remarkable carved and moulded interiors, to the sheer massiveness of her component parts, to her technical features based on cutting-edge maritime technology. Yet, despite design and workmanship that led to her being branded by some as "unsinkable", she took more than 1,500 passengers to watery graves after only five days of her maiden voyage, the result of a collision with an iceberg in the North Atlantic.

Just as *Titanic* had been viewed as the greatest of ships, so did her demise become considered the greatest of maritime disasters. In the days following her loss, the tragedy developed into one of the most sensational newspaper stories of all time, and helped establish the unparalleled reputation for news reporting since enjoyed by *The New York Times*. Her brief life has ever since been the subject of uncountable books, articles, films and other productions.

Even after three-quarters of a century, *Titanic* has proven to be one of the most riveting stories in the world, such as when a team of specialists headed by Robert Ballard of Woods Hole Oceanographic Institution in Massachusetts and Jean-Louis Michel of the Institut français de recherche pour l'exploitation des la mer finally discovered her resting place and returned with photographs of her remains. More sensation was created in the following years when items began to be retrieved from around and even within the ship, and courts ruled her salvage rights to belong to RMS Titanic, Inc.

As recently as 2007, *Titanic* was still reaching the headlines, when, for example, the key for the binocular store on her crow's nest went to auction, or when Barbara West Dainton, the next-to-last survivor of the tragedy, died at the age of 96.

Today, there remains a constant enthusiasm for stories of her background, building, maiden voyage and sinking. Equally as passionately reviewed are the details of those men, women and children aboard her; of the other ships involved in the rescue (or not) of the survivors; of the official inquiries into the tragedy; and of her subsequent discovery and salvage. With numerous museums, societies and websites around the world dedicated to her story and her memory, there is no doubt that her place in history is secure, and no reason to think that *Titanic* will not continue to be a topic of discussion, research and speculation for years to come.

Neither this volume nor any other likely will ever be the "last word" on *Titanic*. New facts and perspectives are regularly being added to the details of her life, fate and aftermath. But this book – as do all of the works in Carlton Books' "Experience" series – adds the special bonus of a wealth of memorabilia, in this case fascinating materials not normally available to the *Titanic* enthusiast. Hopefully, these will help the reader understand more clearly the luxury and splendour of this grandest of ships and the magnitude of her tragedy.

Beau Riffenburgh

The Age of the Liner

The era of *Titanic* marked the apogee of transatlantic luxury cruising. In a time before air travel, the grand ocean liner was the most impressive and luxurious form of transportation in the world, the embodiment of both opulence and man's continuing achievement. But the ships that plied the oceans were also the result of competition founded on the burning desire for financial profits.

In 1839, Samuel Cunard won a contract with the British government to provide a fortnightly mail service from Liverpool to Halifax and Boston. Within a year, the Cunard Line had produced *Britannia*, the first purpose-built ocean

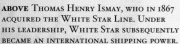

ABOVE THOMAS HENRY ISMAY, WHO IN 1867 ACQUIRED THE WHITE STAR LINE. UNDER HIS LEADERSHIP, WHITE STAR SUBSEQUENTLY BECAME AN INTERNATIONAL SHIPPING POWER.

liner. Soon afterwards, other new Cunard ships – *Acadia*, *Caledonia* and *Columbia* – joined *Britannia* in the first regularly scheduled steamship service to North America, taking approximately 14 days for the passage. For the next three decades, the Cunard Line remained virtually unchallenged.

Meanwhile, the White Star Line, which was founded in the 1840s, developed a strong business taking immigrants to Australia. Within a couple of decades, however, White Star had fallen on hard times, and in 1867 it was taken over by Thomas Henry Ismay. It was not long before Ismay and several colleagues had transformed the company, replacing the old wooden clippers with new iron steamers and entering the Atlantic market. They soon formed a business partnership with renowned Belfast shipbuilder Harland & Wolff, which agreed to construct all of White Star's ships.

The first product of the new alliance, *Oceanic*, appeared in 1871, with numerous design improvements. Within a few years, White Star's *Adriatic*, *Baltic* and *Germanic* had successively won the Blue Riband, the prize awarded to the ship making the fastest crossing of the North Atlantic, and the journey time had dropped to less than seven and a half days. For the next 20 years, Cunard and White Star battled for supremacy, each successively making faster and more advanced ships to accommodate the increasing number of passengers crossing the Atlantic.

BOTTOM LEFT AND BACKGROUND NEAR AN OLD NAVAL SAILING VESSEL IS WHITE STAR'S *CELTIC*. ALTHOUGH NOT AS LONG AS *OCEANIC II*, AT 19,051 TONNES (21,000 TONS) *CELTIC* WAS THE WORLD'S LARGEST SHIP IN 1901.

BELOW ONE OF THE LOUNGES ON *KAISER WILHELM DER GROSSE*. WITH INTERIORS DECORATED IN BAROQUE REVIVAL STYLE, THE GERMAN SHIP WAS THE MOST PLUSH AND ORNATE YET LAUNCHED.

Ship (Line)	Tonnes (Tons)	Knots (Direction)	Period held
City of Paris (*Inman*)	9,525 (10,499)	19.95 (WB) 20.03 (EB) 20.48 (WB) 20.70 (WB)	1889 1889–91 1892 1892–93
Campania (*Cunard*)	11,748 (12,950)	21.30 (EB) 21.44 (WB)	1893–94 1894
Lucania (*Cunard*)	11,750 (12,952)	21.81 (EB) 21.90 (EB) 22.00 (EB)	1894 1894–95 1895–97
Kaiser Wilhelm der Grosse (*NDL*)	13,017 (14,349)	22.33 (EB)	1897–99
Lusitania (*Cunard*)	28,622 (31,550)	23.99 (WB) 23.61 (EB)	1907 1907
Mauretania (*Cunard*)	28,974 (31,938)	24.42 (EB) 25.16 (EB) 25.61 (EB) 25.70 (EB) 25.88 (EB) 26.06 (WB)	1908 1909 1909 1909 1909 1909–29
Normandie (*CGT*)	71,922 (79,280)	29.98 (WB) 30.31 (EB) 30.99 (EB) 31.20 (EB)	1935 1935–36 1937 1937

Largest and Fastest

City of New York *and* City of Paris *were stunning achievements because they were the first liners weighing more than 9,072 tonnes (10,000 tons), while also having the speed to gain the Blue Riband. The following ships are those that held the distinction of being the world's largest liner at the same time as holding the speed record for crossing the Atlantic.*

NDL = Norddeutscher Lloyd
CGT = Compagnie Générale Transatlantique
WB = westbound; EB = eastbound

White Star's challenge to Cunard did not go unnoticed. In 1888, the Inman and International Line launched *City of New York* and *City of Paris*. These were not only extremely elegant, but their twin screws eliminated the need for sails while allowing them to be the first ships to cross the Atlantic eastbound at an average of more than 20 knots. Cunard and White Star quickly responded. White Star emphasized passenger comfort, with Harland & Wolff's chief designer Alexander Carlisle producing *Teutonic* and *Majestic*, the first modern liners. These were ships without sails and with a much greater deck space; accommodation was situated at midships rather than at the stern, where engine noise and vibration were problems.

Meanwhile, Cunard's focus was primarily on speed rather than glamour. In 1893, the company introduced two new ships, *Campania* and *Lucania*, which promptly won back the Blue Riband.

New competition soon appeared from the Germans, highlighted in 1897 when Norddeutscher Lloyd produced *Kaiser Wilhelm der Grosse*. She was the largest, longest and fastest ship afloat, and one that sported four funnels: a new look that would dominate the years to come.

Not everyone was enamoured of such rivalry, however, as fierce competition did not lead to the greatest revenue. One man determined to put profit first was American financier John Pierpont Morgan. Morgan's goal was to set up an alliance of shipping companies under one banner, allowing them to set rates and eliminate expensive advertising and other competitive costs, thus increasing profits. Between 1900 and 1902, Morgan's investment house and several of his business associates orchestrated a series of mergers and share sales that allowed what became the International Mercantile Marine Company (IMMC) to take control of a number of American and British shipping lines. The jewel in Morgan's new shipping crown was the White Star Line. Shortly thereafter, a cooperative pact was established with the main German shipping lines. The only major player that now stood in the way of the IMMC having complete domination of the Atlantic passenger trade was Cunard.

ABOVE LAUNCHED IN 1888, *CITY OF NEW YORK* HAD THREE MASTS, BUT NEVER USED SAILS OWING TO HER INNOVATIVE TWIN SCREWS. TRANSFERRED TO THE AMERICAN LINE, HER NAME WAS SHORTENED TO *NEW YORK*.

BELOW RIGHT WHITE STAR'S *CEDRIC*, FROM WILLS' CIGARETTE CARD SERIES "MERCHANT SHIPS OF THE WORLD". TEN YEARS AFTER HER 1902 LAUNCH, *CEDRIC* TOOK MUCH OF *TITANIC'S* SURVIVING CREW BACK TO BRITAIN.

BOTTOM CHARLES DIXON'S PAINTING OF THE 1899 LAUNCH OF *OCEANIC II*. WHITE STAR'S NEW SHIP SURPASSED *GREAT EASTERN* AS THE LONGEST SHIP YET BUILT.

J P MORGAN

Although John Pierpont Morgan played a key role in the transatlantic passenger trade, ships were only a small part of his economic empire. The son of a banker, in 1861 Morgan started his own bank, and began forming syndicates to underwrite the finances of new companies. In the following years he made a fortune and gained considerable influence over the American economy by financing, reorganizing and merging railroad companies and then the steel industry. He died in Rome, while returning from Egypt, the year after Titanic *sank.*

WILLS'S CIGARETTES.

S.S. CEDRIC.

Fig.1.

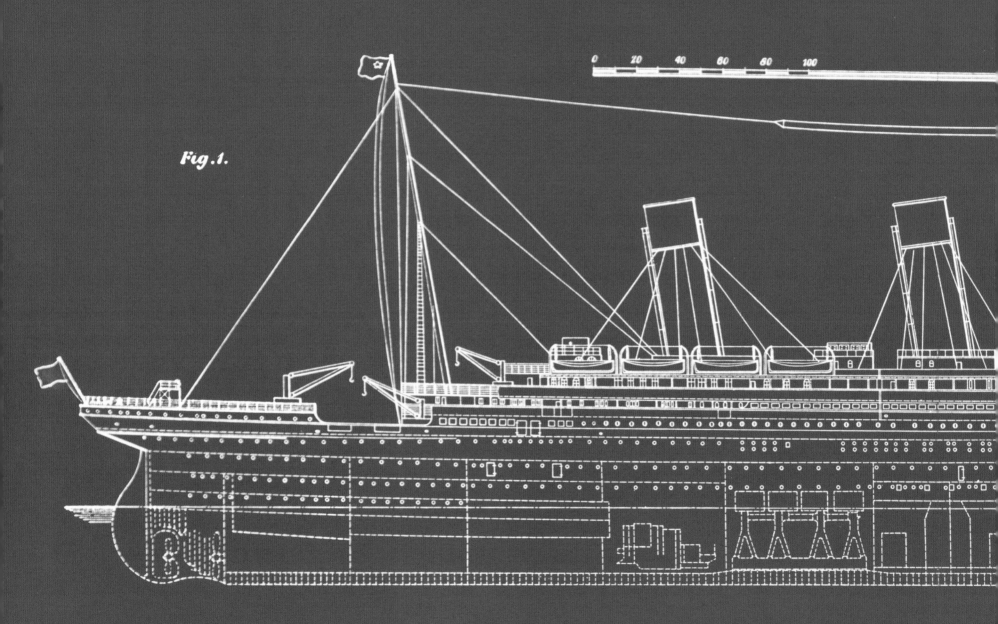

300 400 Feet

BOAT DECK
A
B
C
D
E
F
LOWER

FIGURE 1:
THE GENERAL ARRANGEMENT
BLUEPRINT OF *TITANIC*, THE MOST
BASIC OF THE MANY BLUEPRINTS THAT
WOULD HAVE CAREFULLY SHOWN
THE DESIGN OF EVERY ASPECT OF THE
SHIP. THE 3-METER- (10-FOOT-) LONG
ORIGINAL BLUEPRINTS OF THE SHIP'S
PLUMBING SYSTEM, WHICH WERE TAKEN
OFF *TITANIC* IN CHERBOURG BY NAVAL
ARCHITECT WILLIAM WILSON, WERE
SOLD AT AUCTION IN 2005 FOR £12,000.

THE CONCEPT

At the beginning of the twentieth century, Cunard, the last major transatlantic shipping line with strictly British ownership, was under threat of takeover by J P Morgan's IMMC, which had already acquired the Dominion Line, Red Star Line, Holland-Amerika Line and, in 1902, the White Star Line. In addition, Cunard ships were being outperformed by Norddeutscher Lloyd's *Kaiser Wilhelm der Grosse* and a new, even faster ship: *Deutschland* of the Hamburg-Amerika Line.

It was clear that Cunard needed faster, more lavish ships to compete with the Germans and the IMMC, but the company did not have the funding, so Lord Inverclyde, Cunard's chairman, turned to the British government for help. Set against a backdrop of British unease with growing German power, he negotiated a multimillion-pound loan and an annual subsidy. In return, Inverclyde guaranteed that he would keep Cunard under British control, that the two new ships Cunard built would bring back

the Blue Riband and that they would be able to be turned into armed cruisers in case of war.

In mid-1907, the first of these two new liners, *Lusitania*, came into service and, although at 28,622 tonnes (31,550 tons) she was the largest ship in the world, her power was so enormous that she quickly regained the Blue Riband in both directions. Before the end of the year, however, her sister, *Mauretania*, replaced her as largest at 28,974 tonnes (31,938 tons), and also earned the Blue Riband for eastbound travel, proving so fast that she held on to the title for the next 22 years.

The IMMC responded to Cunard's challenge that very year. On the death of his father in 1899, J Bruce Ismay had become chairman and managing director of the White Star Line. He had kept his position when the company had been taken over, then in 1904 had become president of the IMMC, although J P Morgan maintained the ultimate power.

In 1907 Ismay and Lord Pirrie, chairman of Belfast shipbuilder Harland & Wolff, decided on a revolutionary course of action that they hoped would regain the initiative from Cunard. Their grand concept was to build two huge liners, with a third to follow later.

ABOVE PASSENGERS ABOARD *LUSITANIA*. NOT ONLY DID THE SHIP HAVE RECORD SPEED, HER VAST SIZE MEANT THAT SHE COULD CARRY MORE THAN 2,100 PASSENGERS.

FAR LEFT *MAURETANIA* ALREADY HELD THE BLUE RIBAND, BUT WHEN HER THREE-BLADED PROPELLERS WERE CHANGED TO FOUR BLADES, SHE PRODUCED A TRANSATLANTIC SPEED RECORD (26.06 KNOTS) THAT LASTED FOR DECADES.

THE COMPETITION

In order that Cunard could put both new ships into service as quickly as possible, Lusitania *and* Mauretania *were built at separate shipyards. This resulted in a competitive spirit that saw the shipbuilders incorporate every innovation they thought might make their respective ship the best. Although they appeared similar on the outside, the interiors contrasted starkly with one another:* Lusitania's *gold leaf on plaster gave it an open, airy feeling, while the oak, mahogany and other dark wood of* Mauretania *produced a more sober, subdued atmosphere. Although* Mauretania *was faster,* Lusitania *ultimately proved more popular with passengers.*

ABOVE WILLIAM PIRRIE JOINED HARLAND & WOLFF AT 15 AS AN APPRENTICE DRAUGHTSMAN. WITHIN A DECADE HE ROSE TO HEAD DESIGNER. EVENTUALLY HE BECAME A PARTNER AND LATER COMPANY CHAIRMAN.

LEFT CUNARD'S *LUSITANIA*, WHICH, AT THE TIME OF HER LAUNCH, WAS THE LARGEST SHIP IN THE WORLD.

LEFT THE GIGANTIC GANTRY OVER THE SLIPWAYS WHERE *Olympic* AND *Titanic* WERE BUILT. IT INCLUDED FOUR HUGE ELECTRIC LIFTS AND A REMARKABLE SERIES OF CRANES.

RIGHT THE 16,000-HORSE-POWER TURBINE ENGINE IN THE PROCESS OF BEING INSTALLED. THIS MASSIVE, LOW-PRESSURE ENGINE DROVE THE 20-TONNE (22-TON), FOUR-BLADED CENTRAL PROPELLER.

BACKGROUND THE SINKING OF *Lusitania* ON 7 MAY 1915. TORPEDOED BY A GERMAN U-BOAT OFF IRELAND, SHE WENT DOWN WITH THE LOSS OF SOME 1,200 LIVES.

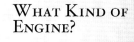

WHAT KIND OF ENGINE?

One of the key questions for shipbuilders at the start of the twentieth century was whether to power ships with traditional, piston-based reciprocating engines or with the more recent steam turbine. Cunard tested this in sister ships brought into service in 1905. Carmania's steam turbine proved faster and more economical than Caronia's reciprocating engine, leading Cunard to put turbines in both Lusitania *and* Mauretania. *Similarly, White Star's* Megantic *used reciprocating engines and her sister* Laurentic *a combination of the two engines. Based on Laurentic's success, combination engines were designed for* Olympic *and* Titanic.

These would dwarf the Cunard ships, being about 30 metres (100 feet) longer and, at 41,730 tonnes (46,000 tons), half as large again. Rather than attempting to equal the speed of *Mauretania*, the new ships would concentrate on elegance, luxury, comfort and safety, while also still being able to complete the Atlantic passage within a week. Even the lower speed would be beneficial, as it would reduce the engine noise and vibration that plagued *Lusitania* and *Mauretania*. Moreover, the new ships would be so large that they would benefit from economy of scale, their unrivalled lavishness appealing to large numbers of first-class passengers, and second- and third-class passengers also finding larger and better facilities than on any other ship.

The only weakness in the plan seemed to be that there was no shipyard in the world with the facilities to produce such mammoths. That did not stop Pirrie, who simply converted three of Harland & Wolff's largest berths into two specially strengthened and lengthened slipways. Over them, William Arrol and Company, builder of the famous Forth Rail Bridge, constructed a gantry that rose 69.5 metres (228 feet) to the upper crane. Measuring 256 by 82.3 metres (840 by 270 feet) and weighing more than 5,443 tonnes (6,000 tons), the gantry was the largest such structure in the world. At the same time, Ismay began discussions with the New York Harbor Board about lengthening

the White Star piers. He was initially refused, but when J P Morgan began pulling strings, the desired permissions eventually came through.

Meanwhile, plans for the first two ships were drawn up by a team at Harland & Wolff, under the guidance of the general manager for design, Alexander Carlisle, Pirrie's brother-in-law. In July 1908, Ismay travelled to Belfast, where he approved the design plans. The building of the largest ships in the world could now commence.

BELOW THE DRAWING OFFICE AT HARLAND & WOLFF, WHERE THE PLANS FOR *TITANIC* WERE PREPARED. THE MANY WINDOWS AND BARREL CEILING PROVIDED THE MAXIMUM AMOUNT OF NATURAL LIGHT.

BELOW RIGHT ALEXANDER CARLISLE, LORD PIRRIE'S BROTHER-IN-LAW, WAS ONE OF THE KEY DESIGNERS OF *TITANIC*, ULTIMATELY BEING RESPONSIBLE FOR THE INTERNAL LAYOUT, DESIGN AND DECORATION.

ENCLOSURE
The original design drawing for *Olympic* and *Titanic*. The plan shows the space given to the boilers and engines, and how the hull was divided into "watertight" compartments. Also shown in background.

WHITE STAR LINE.

"OLYMPIC." 45,000 TONS.
AND
"TITANIC." 45,000 TONS.

THE LARGEST STEAMERS IN THE WORLD.

To NEW YORK,
From SOUTHAMPTON–CHERBOURG–QUEENSTOWN.
From LIVERPOOL–QUEENSTOWN.

To BOSTON.
From LIVERPOOL–QUEENSTOWN.

For Freight and Passage apply to

THOS. COOK & SON.

31, Fargate, SHEFFIELD;
16, Clumber Street and
97, Derby Road, NOTTINGHAM;
and Gallowtree Gate, LEICESTER.

ABOVE An advertisement for passage to New York or Boston on the White Star Line ships *Olympic* and *Titanic*, with arrangements to be made through Thomas Cook.

BELOW *Titanic* in the process of receiving the plates for her hull. Immediately adjacent to her was *Olympic*.

Building the Biggest Ships in the World

The first task that now faced Harland & Wolff was to develop the infrastructure that would allow the monster ships to be built. Throughout the latter half of 1908, the two new giant slipways were prepared and the gantry constructed high above them. Finally, on 16 December 1908 at Slip Two, the first keel plate was laid for what would become *Olympic*. Then, on 31 March 1909, next door at Slip Three, a similar keel began to be laid. It was Harland & Wolff's keel number 401, and the ship that would rise from it would become known as *Titanic*.

The two ships were virtually identical in their initial construction. Up from the keel rose powerful frames that were set from 0.6–1 metre (2–3 feet) apart and were held in place by a series of steel beams and girders. Steel plates up to 11 metres (36 feet) long were riveted on the outside of the frames. Each ship had a double bottom, comprising an outer skin of 2.5-centimetres- (1-inch-) thick steel plates and a slightly less heavy inner skin. This was a safety measure designed to keep the ship afloat if the outer skin was punctured. So massive was the double bottom that a man could walk upright in the area between the skins. To hold all this together, more than half a million iron rivets were used on these lower reaches of *Titanic*, some areas even being quadruple-riveted. By the time the ship was complete, more than three million rivets had been used.

The original plans produced by the design group under Alexander Carlisle reflected the latest thinking in marine architecture. The hull, for example, was divided into 16 compartments formed by 15 watertight transverse bulkheads. It was believed these made the ships essentially unsinkable, as it was claimed they could float with any two of these compartments flooded. However, the bulkheads were built as a protection against the kind of accident that had occurred in 1879, when the Guion Line's *Arizona* had rammed an iceberg in

OPPOSITE RIGHT Lord Pirrie and J Bruce Ismay making a final inspection of *Titanic* shortly before her launch. Next to them is a pressure gauge for the hydraulic launching trigger.

BACKGROUND Workmen pour out of the shipyard after a shift ends. Of Harland & Wolff's 15,000 employees, more than 3,000 were working on *Titanic* at any one time.

BELOW The vast hull of *Titanic* shortly after it was launched.

The Launching of Titanic

The launching of Titanic *was a momentous occasion, with an estimated 100,000 people – one-third of Belfast – turning out to watch. J P Morgan, who had come from New York for the occasion, arrived on the chartered steamer* Duke of Argyll, *along with special guests and more than 100 reporters from England. Shortly before 12:15pm, Lord Pirrie ordered the last timber supports to be knocked away. Moving under her own weight, in 62 seconds the 21,772-tonne (24,000-ton) hull slid down a slipway greased with 20 tonnes (22 tons) of tallow, soap and train oil. As thousands cheered, the hull slipped through the water until being stopped by special anchors.*

WHITE STAR
ROYAL MAIL STEAMER
"TITANIC."

the fog. Although the bow of *Arizona* was virtually destroyed, the collision bulkheads had prevented her from sinking and she had been able to steam back to St John's, Newfoundland, stern-first. Thus, to many, *Titanic* seemed invincible because her extensive bulkhead system protected her from similar damage; unfortunately, however, it did little to protect the enormously long sides that proved to be her most vulnerable region.

Throughout 1909 and into 1910, more than 4,000 employees of Harland & Wolff worked on *Olympic* and *Titanic*. When Carlisle retired in 1910, he was succeeded by Pirrie's nephew, Thomas Andrews. Finally, in October 1910, *Olympic* was launched and towed to her fitting-out basin to be completed. Work also continued on *Titanic*, and on 31 May 1911, the same day *Olympic* was handed over to the White Star Line, the hull of *Titanic* was launched. Her dimensions were staggering. If placed on end, she would have been taller than any building in the world at the time:

269.1 metres (882 feet) – about four New York City blocks. Even sitting upright she would be as high as an 11-storey building.

After the launch, the hull of *Titanic* was towed to a deep-water wharf, where, during the following months, a giant floating crane was used to load engines, boilers, electrical generators, refrigeration equipment and all of the other heavy machinery needed to run what would effectively become a small town. She received three anchors totalling 28 tonnes (31 tons), eight electric cargo cranes and, far above, four funnels – the three front ones were connected to the boiler rooms, with a dummy aft funnel positioned over the turbine room, to which it supplied ventilation. Carlisle's original plans included only three funnels, but the fourth had been added to enhance the lines of the ship. Each was so vast that a train could be driven through it. With the basic equipment in place, many more months were spent outfitting and detailing, producing what was widely considered the most impressive ship in the world.

BELOW *TITANIC* DURING FITTING-OUT AT THE THOMPSON DOCK IN BELFAST. ON 8 MARCH 1912 SHE WAS TOWED FROM THE DRY DOCK FOR THE FINAL DEEPWATER FITTING-OUT.

TITANIC'S SPECIFICATIONS

LENGTH:	269.06 metres (882 feet, 9 inches)
BEAM:	28.19 metres (92 feet, 6 inches)
MOULDED DEPTH:	18.13 metres (59 feet, 6 inches)
TONNAGE	46,329 gross; 21,831 net
PASSENGER DECKS:	7
BOILERS	29
BOILER FURNACES:	162
ENGINES:	Two four-cylinder, triple expansion reciprocating of 15,000 hp apiece, one low-pressure steam turbine of 16,000 hp
SPEED:	Service, 21 knots; max, approximately 23–24 knots
MAX PASSENGERS AND CREW:	2,603 passengers, 944 crew
LIFEBOATS:	16 + 4 collapsible (1,178 capacity)

ABOVE IT TOOK A WHOLE TEAM OF HORSES TO PULL THE SPECIALLY BUILT CART HOLDING ONE OF THE 14-TONNE (15½-TON) ANCHORS NEEDED FOR *TITANIC*.

LEFT THE FUNNELS OF *TITANIC* WERE COMPARABLE TO OTHER PARTS OF THE SHIP IN THAT THEIR SHEER SIZE WAS SIMPLY OVERWHELMING.

The Glamour of Titanic

By the end of her outfitting, *Titanic* had become the most luxurious and elegant ship in the world, and one that could not fail to impress. The designers had even learned from the early voyages of *Olympic*, following which *Titanic* received several alterations before going into service. The major change to the exterior was the addition of a glass canopy with sliding windows along the first-class promenade on A deck, so that the passengers would be protected from bad weather and sea spray.

The interior was extravagantly grand, and first-class passengers were treated to staterooms, public rooms, fittings and furnishings, and food that could be expected from the finest hotels

and restaurants in the world. Yet although the ship was strictly segregated by class, it was as impressive for those in second- and third-class as for the wealthier passengers. In fact, second-class bettered that of first-class on most other liners, while

third-class surpassed the accommodation and amenities of second-class on other ships.

Each class had its own dining saloons, smoking rooms, lounges or libraries, stairways and promenades. In addition to three first-class elevators, there was one for second-class: a first on any ship. Nothing was more spectacular than the forward grand staircase (there was also a similar one aft), which was covered by a massive glass dome and extended downwards for five levels, from the first-class entrance on the boat deck to E deck, the lowest level on which there were first-class cabins.

Accommodation on A, B and C decks was reserved for first-class passengers, who were also able to enjoy luxurious reading rooms, a palm court, gymnasium, swimming pool, squash court, Turkish baths, their own barber shop and even ivy growing on trellised walls.

The first-class staterooms were decorated in the style of different design periods, including Italian Renaissance, Louis XIV, Georgian, Queen Anne and current Empire. They varied from one to three berths, and some incorporated an adjoining or nearby cabin for a personal

ABOVE An illustration from a White Star Line brochure of the time, showing how the swimming pool aboard *Titanic* was supposed to look.

BACKGROUND The real first-class staircase aboard *Titanic*.

RIGHT A drawing of a first-class parlour suite. Suites like this were found on both *Titanic* and *Olympic*.

ABOVE An illustration of the first-class staircase aboard *Titanic* and its opulent surroundings. There were actually two of these remarkable masterpieces.

OPPOSITE BOTTOM The first-class dining saloon was advertised as the largest room afloat. This remarkable venue could seat 550 people and included Jacobean-style alcoves along the sides.

OPPOSITE TOP LEFT A china serving plate and a cup and saucer from *Titanic*, an example of the fine crockery used by diners aboard the ship.

First-Class Suites

There were numerous first-class suites on Titanic, *but the most expensive were the four parlour suites on decks B and C. Each of these had a sitting room, two bedrooms, two wardrobe rooms and a private bath and lavatory. Thomas Drake Cardeza and his mother Charlotte occupied the suite on the starboard side of B deck, paying £512 6s 7d, the most for any passengers aboard; this price also included cabins for their two servants. On the port side, opposite the Cardezas, J Bruce Ismay's suite included its own private 15.2-metre (50-foot) promenade.*

separated – men in the bow and women in the stern. The first-class dining saloon was the largest room on *Titanic*, extending 34.7 metres (114 feet) for the entire width of the ship, and catering for 550 people at a time. First-class passengers could also enjoy an à la carte restaurant, the Verandah Café at the palm court or the Café Parisien, which quickly became a favourite with the younger set. On D deck, the second-class dining saloon, which could seat 394 people, was panelled in oak, like the second-class smoking room, whereas the large second-class lounge featured sycamore panelling and upholstered mahogany chairs. For third-class dining, there was a 30.5-metre- (100-feet-) long saloon on F deck. Seating 473 passengers, it was relatively basic, and was divided in two by a watertight bulkhead. However, compared with the dining arrangements on other ships, where long, bolted-down benches and crowded quarters were the order of the day, it was vastly superior, featuring smaller tables as well as the luxury of separate chairs.

servant. Many of the first-class staterooms were en suite, but some of the less expensive ones (they varied between £263 and £25 11s 9d) shared a washroom. The 207 second-class cabins, located on decks D, E, F and G, were serviced by their own splendid staircase, and consisted of mahogany furniture in two-, three- or four-berth cabins set off oak-panelled corridors that were carpeted in red or green. Many ships housed third-class immigrants in open berths in large, dormitory-style rooms; although *Titanic* did have some of these (the least expensive fare was less than £7), there were also 222 third-class cabins with pine panelling and attractive floor coverings. For those who were housed in the dormitories, single men and women were kept well

BELOW MENUS SHOWING THE KIND OF FOOD PASSENGERS COULD EXPECT. THE FIRST-CLASS MENU (LEFT) IS FROM THE DATE OF DEPARTURE FROM SOUTHAMPTON, AND THE SECOND-CLASS ONE (RIGHT) IS FROM THE LAST DINNER SERVED ABOARD *TITANIC*. SECOND-CLASS FARE, LIKE THE RESTAURANT ITSELF, WAS OF MUCH HIGHER QUALITY THAN ON MOST OTHER SHIPS.

FOOD LOADED ABOARD TITANIC

The food loaded aboard Titanic *in Southampton prior to departure for the week-long trip included:*

FOOD	WEIGHT
Fresh meat	34,000 kg (75,000 lb)
Poultry & game	11,350 kg (25,000 lb)
Fresh fish	5,000 kg (11,000 lb)
Bacon & ham	3,400 kg (7,500 lb)
Salt & dried fish	1,815 kg (4,000 lb)
Sausages	1,135 kg (2,500 lb)
Eggs	40,000
Potatoes	35.7 tonnes (40 tons)
Rice & dried beans	4,540 kg (10,000 lb)
Cereals	4,540 kg (10,000 lb)
Sugar	4,540 kg (10,000 lb)
Flour	200 barrels
Fresh butter	2,725 kg (6,000 lb)
Fresh milk	5,678 litres (1,500 gallons)
Condensed milk	2,271 litres (600 gallons)
Onions	1,600 kg (3,500 lb)
Oranges	36,000
Lemons	16,000
Lettuce	7,000 heads
Tomatoes	2.4 tonnes (2.75 tons)
Green peas	1,020 kg (2,250 lb)
Asparagus	800 bundles
Coffee	1,000 kg (2,200 lb)
Tea	360 kg (800 lb)
Beer	20,000 bottles
Wine	1,500 bottles

Although *Titanic* was certainly magnificent in terms of cabins and public rooms, she was perhaps even more remarkable in areas passengers never saw. Her propulsion came mainly from two four-cylinder, triple-expansion reciprocating engines sending 15,000 horsepower apiece to the massive 34-tonne (38-ton), three-bladed wing propellers. In addition, a 381-tonne (420-ton), low-pressure turbine recycled steam from the other engines, providing 16,000 horsepower to drive the 20 tonne (22-ton), four-bladed, manganese-bronze centre propeller, which had been cast in one piece. This allowed her a projected top speed of approximately 24 knots.

There were 29 gigantic boilers, most measuring 6.1 metres long by 4.8 metres in diameter (20 feet by 15 feet 9 inches), providing the steam for these engines, at a pressure of 15 kilograms per square centimetre (215 pounds per square inch). The boilers were driven by 162 coal furnaces that were stoked continually by a team of firemen, or stokers, numbering approximately 175. An average of approximately 544 tonnes (600 tons) of coal was consumed daily from bunkers holding more than 7,257 tonnes (8,000 tons), and an additional 70 "trimmers" were employed to bring it from the bunkers to the firemen at the furnaces.

The figures were just as amazing for other technical features throughout the colossal ship. The cast-steel rudder was constructed in six pieces, which together measured 24 metres long by 4.6 metres wide (78 feet 8 inches by 15 feet 3 inches), and weighed more than 91 tonnes (100 tons).

Titanic also benefited from electricity to an extent highly unusual at the time. The main generating plant consisted of four 400-kilowatt, steam-powered generators, which produced 16,000 amps at 100 volts: a total that matched many stations in British cities. But such power was absolutely required because there were no fewer than 150 electric motors, complete with hundreds of miles of wire and cable. These serviced 10,000 incandescent lamps, 1,500 bells used to call stewards, 520 electric heaters, a telephone exchange of 50 lines and uncountable passenger signs, lifts, cranes, winches, fans, workshop tools, kitchen and pantry appliances and navigational aids.

ABOVE A group of workmen from Harland & Wolff are dwarfed by the giant wing propellers shortly before *Titanic* was launched.

BACKGROUND The massive triple propeller arrangement that, with a total of 46,000 horsepower being sent to it, could drive *Titanic* at up to 24 knots.

OPPOSITE RIGHT The starboard anchor approaches the surface as it is raised for the final time. Also evident is the massive side plating that was used in *Titanic*'s construction.

LEFT One of the steam engines, as assembled at Harland & Wolff in May 1911. It was subsequently dismantled and then reassembled aboard *Titanic*.

RIGHT A watertight door that was a key safety feature aboard *Titanic*.

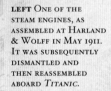

The Watertight Doors

Another design feature that led to Titanic being considered unsinkable was the set of massive watertight doors linking the 15 supposedly watertight compartments. These doors, extending through each bulkhead, were normally held open by a friction clutch. In an emergency, the clutch could, in theory, be released by the captain using a control panel on the bridge. Each door could also be closed individually at its location. Finally, each door was equipped with a float mechanism that would automatically lift and trip a switch to close the door if water entered that compartment.

The main plant was also the primary power source for the Marconi wireless telegraphy station. With two dedicated operators, the wireless station was located on the boat deck, where it was linked to a double aerial that ran between the two masts more than 61 metres (200 feet) above the water surface. Considered a key safety feature, it had alternative sources of power should the main electricity go down, including storage batteries directly in the operating room.

The generating plant also powered two refrigeration engines, which in turn drove a host of cold rooms. Separate accommodation was provided for different kinds of meat, fish, vegetables, fruit, milk and butter, beer, champagne, flowers, chocolate and eggs. Perishable cargo was also housed in cool areas near the main provision stores, and cold pantries and larders, ice-makers and water coolers were placed around the ship, where stewards could meet passengers' needs easily.

Even the three-part bronze whistles aboard *Titanic* were something special. Weighing about 340 kilograms (750 pounds) each and standing

ATTACHMENT
A surveyor's certificate confirming that, as required by the Merchant Shipping Act of 1894, specific spaces on *Titanic* had been inspected, conformed to mandatory standards and could not be used for any other purposes.

ABOVE The painting *Men of Iron* by William Conor of Belfast. Shipyard workers watch a ship waiting to be launched from below the giant gantry.

RIGHT The lifeboats held by their Welin davits at a time when no one expected them to be used.

BOTTOM RIGHT Shipyard workers fitting the starboard tail shaft in May 1911, prior to launch. The gigantic rudder can be seen on the left.

more than 1.2 metres (four feet) high, they were the largest whistles ever aboard a ship. They were powered by steam via an automated whistle-blowing system that used three chambers with diameters of 38.1, 30.5 and 22.9 centimetres, (15, 12 and 9 inches) for a variation of sound that combined into one sustained blast.

Because of the size and complexity of the ship, communication throughout it had been carefully considered. The boiler rooms, for example, were linked to the starting platform by a series of illuminated telegraphs, allowing the engineer to communicate with them swiftly and efficiently. Overall, the technological achievements of *Titanic* were so imposing that, as completion approached, the trade journal *The Shipbuilder* was able to state she was "practically unsinkable".

WHY WERE THERE SO FEW LIFEBOATS?

In 1894, British Board of Trade regulations were established that required all British ships of more than 9,072 tonnes (10,000 tons) to carry 16 lifeboats able to provide space for 962 people. This had not been unreasonable as, at 12,952 tons, Lucania was the largest ship in the world. Eighteen years later, however, these regulations had not been updated, despite the fact that at more than 41,730 tonnes (46,000 tons) Titanic could take four times that many passengers and crew. Alexander Carlisle was well aware of such safety issues, and his original design planned for Titanic to have 64 lifeboats – enough to carry all passengers and crew. However, key figures at the White Star Line or the IMMC insisted on larger promenades, which were gained at the expense of the lifeboats. Carlisle's arguments were overridden, and he was forced to decrease the number of lifeboats to 40, then 32, then finally 16 – with tragic consequences.

THE UNSINKABLE SHIP

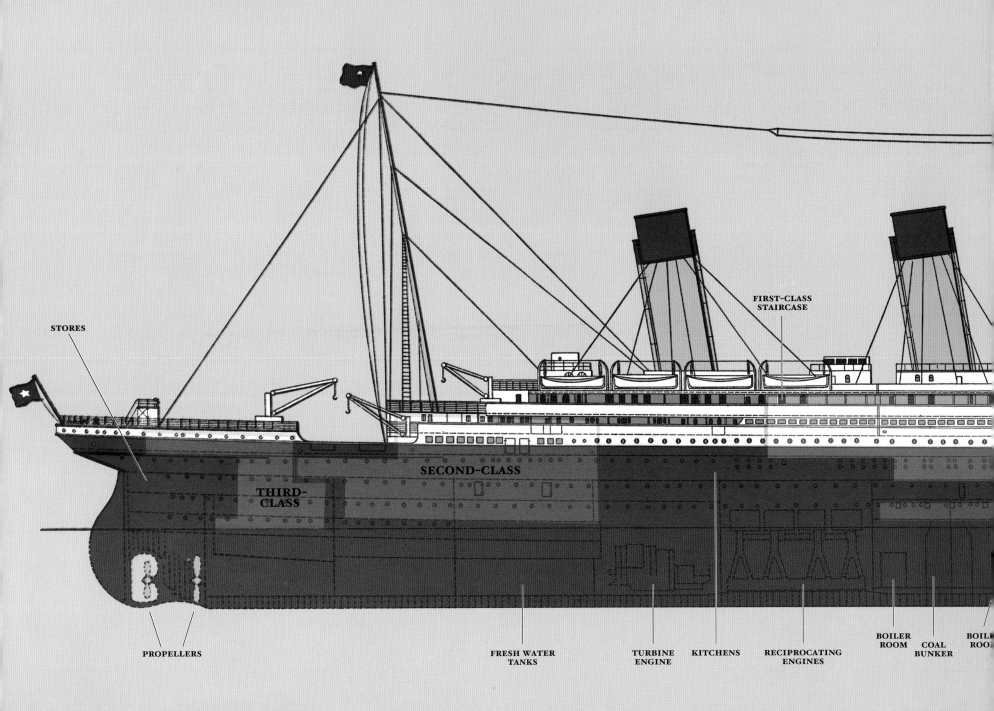

STORES

FIRST-CLASS
STAIRCASE

SECOND-CLASS

THIRD-
CLASS

PROPELLERS

FRESH WATER
TANKS

TURBINE
ENGINE

KITCHENS

RECIPROCATING
ENGINES

BOILER
ROOM

COAL
BUNKER

BOILER
ROOM

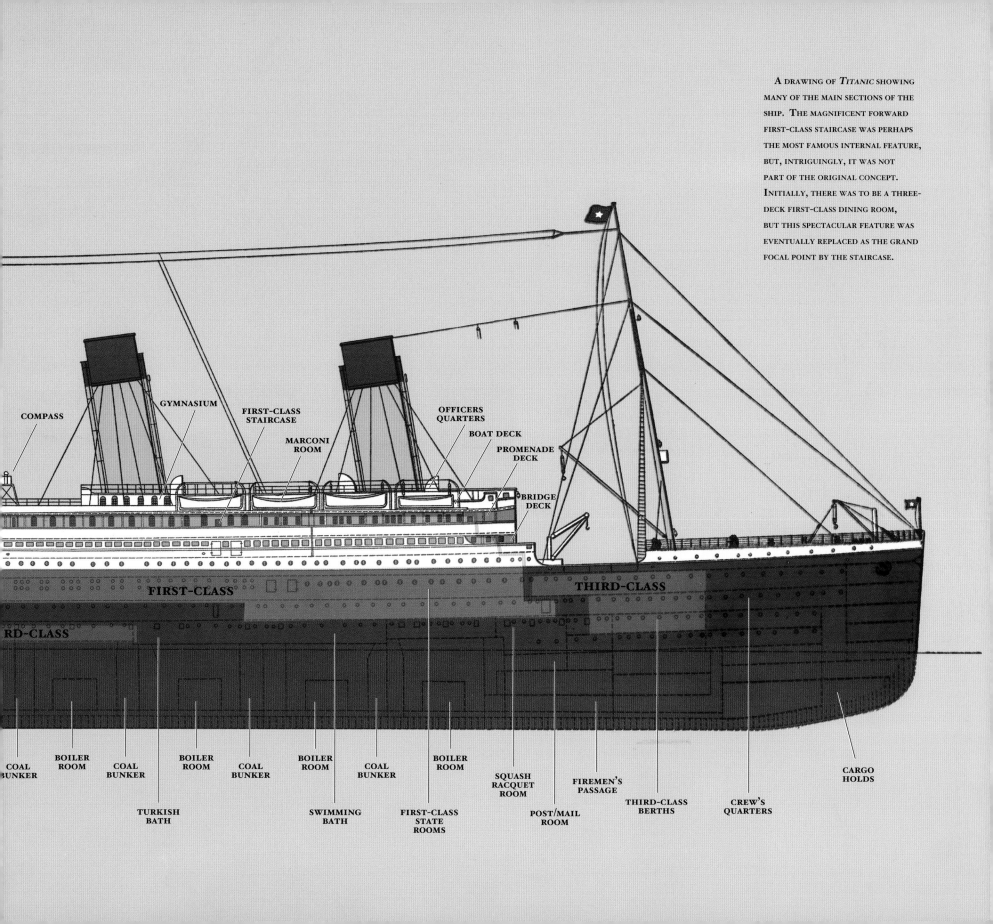

A DRAWING OF *TITANIC* SHOWING
MANY OF THE MAIN SECTIONS OF THE
SHIP. THE MAGNIFICENT FORWARD
FIRST-CLASS STAIRCASE WAS PERHAPS
THE MOST FAMOUS INTERNAL FEATURE,
BUT, INTRIGUINGLY, IT WAS NOT
PART OF THE ORIGINAL CONCEPT.
INITIALLY, THERE WAS TO BE A THREE-
DECK FIRST-CLASS DINING ROOM,
BUT THIS SPECTACULAR FEATURE WAS
EVENTUALLY REPLACED AS THE GRAND
FOCAL POINT BY THE STAIRCASE.

COMPASS

GYMNASIUM

FIRST-CLASS
STAIRCASE

MARCONI
ROOM

OFFICERS
QUARTERS

BOAT DECK

PROMENADE
DECK

BRIDGE
DECK

FIRST-CLASS

THIRD-CLASS

RD-CLASS

COAL
BUNKER

BOILER
ROOM

COAL
BUNKER

BOILER
ROOM

COAL
BUNKER

BOILER
ROOM

COAL
BUNKER

BOILER
ROOM

SQUASH
RACQUET
ROOM

FIREMEN'S
PASSAGE

CARGO
HOLDS

TURKISH
BATH

SWIMMING
BATH

FIRST-CLASS
STATE
ROOMS

POST/MAIL
ROOM

THIRD-CLASS
BERTHS

CREW'S
QUARTERS

A NEW COMMAND

There was never any doubt who would captain *Titanic* during her maiden voyage. Edward J Smith had joined the White Star Line in 1880 as fourth officer of *Celtic*. By 1887, he had earned his first command, and in 1904 he was made commodore of White Star's fleet, for which he generally thereafter commanded the new ships on their first cruises. Smith looked every part the rugged ship's master, but he was also calm, soft-spoken and had such a reassuring disposition that many passengers would only go to sea with him as captain. His crews had equal confidence in him.

In June 1911, Smith took *Olympic* on her first transatlantic cruise, the success of which was offset only by an incident in New York Harbor, when the forces from the huge ship's water displacement pulled the tug *Hallenbeck* under her stern, severely damaging the smaller ship. A similar incident occurred several months

later, when HMS *Hawke* collided with *Olympic*, which again was under the command of Captain Smith. These two accidents notwithstanding, when the fitting-out of *Titanic* was finished, it was Smith who was placed in command.

On 2 April 1912, having been delayed one day by bad weather, *Titanic* was put through her sea trials. Aboard were 41 officers and senior crew and 78 men from the "black gang": stokers, trimmers and greasers. Harold Sanderson represented the White

COLLISION WITH HMS *Hawke*

Even a master with Edward Smith's experience had much to learn about handling giant liners. On 20 September 1911, Olympic departed from Southampton on her fifth voyage. After sailing on a course parallel to HMS Hawke, Olympic turned, and the 6,804-tonne (7,500-ton) naval cruiser rammed into her, puncturing her in two places. It was later determined that dynamic forces caused by massive water displacement had pulled Hawke into Olympic, and the harbour pilot, rather than Smith, received the official blame. Meanwhile, Olympic's repairs in Belfast assumed priority over work on Titanic, thereby delaying Titanic's first cruise for three weeks.

LEFT PURSER HUGH MCELROY AND CAPTAIN EDWARD J SMITH ABOARD *TITANIC* BEFORE HER FINAL STOP AT QUEENSTOWN, IRELAND. NEITHER MAN SURVIVED THE TRAGEDY.

ABOVE ONE OF THE BIGGEST TASKS FOR THE CREW IN PORT WAS TO BRING ABOARD AND UNLOAD THE POST. ALSO SHOWN IS A CREWMAN ADJUSTING A LANTERN.

RIGHT INTERESTED BYSTANDERS WATCH AS WORKMEN INVESTIGATE THE DAMAGE TO *OLYMPIC* CAUSED BY THE COLLISION WITH HMS *HAWKE*. BOTH SHIPS WERE SERIOUSLY DAMAGED, BUT NO PEOPLE WERE INJURED.

BACKGROUND IN CHARGE OF THE GYMNASIUM WAS PHYSICAL INSTRUCTOR T W MCCAWLEY OF ABERDEEN, WHO DEMONSTRATED TO FATHER BROWNE HOW TO USE A ROWING MACHINE.

Star Line and Thomas Andrews was there for Harland & Wolff, as was his "Guarantee Group": a select company of eight enthusiastic and extremely talented men who went on maiden voyages to resolve any problems that arose. Throughout the day, *Titanic*'s speed, turning and manoeuvring capability, stopping distance, reversing and many other functions, including wireless, anchors and electrical systems, were tested. That evening, she was approved by the Board of Trade and transferred over to White Star.

Intriguingly, this approval was given despite a fire smouldering in a boiler-room coal bunker. Although fire is normally the most feared danger aboard ship, the problem could not be immediately controlled, and it was a number of days before the bunker had been emptied to the extent that the seat of the blaze could be extinguished.

At 8pm, after boarding fresh provisions, *Titanic* left Belfast for the last time, steaming for Southampton. En route, she reached a speed of 23¼ knots – the fastest she would ever go. When she arrived at Southampton shortly before midnight on 3 April, she swung round and, with the help of several tugs, approached the dock stern-first. She would thus be able to make an impressive departure without having to turn while leaving. There were now only six days for provisioning and staffing, and for making any final touches in preparation for the maiden voyage. One of the most demanding tasks was coaling, because a national coal strike ended only on 6 April, four days before her scheduled departure. With no time for coal to arrive from the pits, White

ABOVE LEFT At the age of 51, chief engineer Joseph Bell was a highly respected professional who had spent about 27 years with White Star Line.

ABOVE Vendors had franchises to sell lace and other souvenirs aboard liners at Queenstown, as shown in one of the last photos from *Titanic*, taken by Father Browne.

Star transferred 4,016 tonnes (4,427 tons) from five other International Mercantile Marine Company ships in port and from the stock remaining after the departure of *Olympic*, which had left only hours before *Titanic* arrived.

One unexpected addition in Southampton was Henry T Wilde, who was named chief officer after having served in the same position aboard *Olympic*. The other officers had joined in Belfast with Captain Smith, but late in the game it was decided that Wilde's knowledge of the vast new liners meant he should be aboard for *Titanic*'s first voyage. The current chief officer, William Murdoch, was dropped to first officer, and first officer Charles Lightoller became the second officer. The third through sixth officers – Herbert Pitman, Joseph Boxhall, Harold Lowe and James Moody – remained the same, while the second officer who had joined in Belfast, David Blair, was reassigned elsewhere, not yet knowing his extremely good fortune.

The Crew of Titanic

Just as there is debate about the exact number of passengers saved and lost on Titanic, *there is no agreement about the exact number of serving crew, although they numbered approximately 890. Recent estimates for the crew by department and position include:*

BELOW Captain Smith (centre, with the white beard) with his senior officers aboard *Titanic*.

Department	Total
Victualling Department	431
Saloon Stewards	130
Bedroom Stewards	47
Stewards	46
Cooks and Bakers	34
Stewardesses	21
Scullions	13
Assistant Saloon Stewards	13
Engine Department	325
Firemen/Stokers	161
Trimmers	72
Greasers	33
Leading Firemen	13
À la Carte Restaurant Department	69
Assistant Waiters	17
Waiters	16
Cooks	15
Deck Department	66
Able Seamen	29

PREMONITIONS OF DISASTER

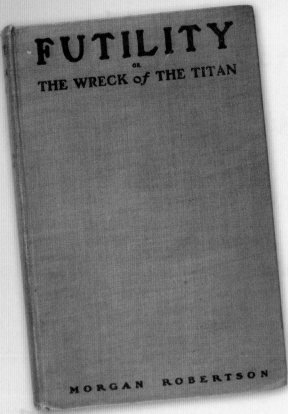

Six years later, in *Review of Reviews*, Stead revisited the theme in another short work of fiction, "From the Old World to the New", in which a clairvoyant aboard White Star's *Majestic* helped to guide a rescue of those aboard another ship that had struck an iceberg in the North Atlantic. Uncannily, the name Stead gave to the captain of *Majestic* was E J Smith – the same name as the captain of *Titanic*. Even stranger, Stead lost his life as a first-class passenger on *Titanic*.

In 1898, 14 years before the tragedy, the former merchant navy officer Morgan Robertson published the novella *The Wreck of the Titan; or, Futility*, in which an "unsinkable" British liner named *Titan*, on a voyage from New York to England, sank with 2,000 people aboard after being tipped on her side in a collision with an iceberg. Not only was the description of *Titan* unnervingly similar to *Titanic* – having roughly the same length, displacement, speed, watertight compartments and number of propellers – but the fictional ship also lacked anywhere near the proper number of lifeboats.

BELOW FATHER FRANK BROWNE AS AN OLDER MAN. HIS LATER PHOTOGRAPHIC ACHIEVEMENTS WERE WIDELY RESPECTED.

BACKGROUND A LETTER FROM HARLAND & WOLFF TO THE BELFAST HARBOUR MASTER COMMENTING ON THE SPEED OF LOCAL STEAMERS CAUSING A SEVERE WASH THAT ENDANGERED WORKERS ABOARD THE STILL-UNFINISHED *TITANIC*.

NO POPE

Although many consider one story that originated during the building of Titanic *to be a myth, it remains one of the most often-repeated tales. It is said that the number 3909 04 was scrawled on the hull as an addition to its official hull number, 401. When this was seen one day as a mirror image, it was noted with horror that it read "NO POPE". Many of the workers in Belfast were Catholic, and it is rumoured that there was great anxiety and concern among them, which later turned to certainty that the ship was destined for disaster.*

Perhaps the eeriest aspect of the *Titanic* disaster was the large number of prophetic tales and premonitions that seemed to foretell its terrible fate. As early as 1886, the famed British journalist W T Stead wrote a fictional story entitled "How the Mail Steamer Went Down in Mid-Atlantic" for his newspaper, *The Pall Mall Gazette*. In the story, a liner sank after colliding with another ship, and most of the people aboard died because of a shortage of lifeboats. At the end of the piece, Stead added: "This is exactly what might take place and will take place if liners are set free short of boats."

ABOVE AN OLD COPY OF MORGAN ROBERTSON'S CLASSIC DISASTER NOVELLA, WHICH WAS ORIGINALLY PUBLISHED WITH THE TWO PARTS OF THE TITLE IN THE REVERSE ORDER.

RIGHT FATHER BROWNE SHOT THIS IMAGE OF CROWDS AT THE WHITE STAR WHARF IN QUEENSTOWN WAITING TO EMBARK THE TENDERS THAT WOULD TAKE THEM TO *TITANIC*.

Equally as bizarre were the numerous portentous events surrounding people sailing on *Titanic*. One of the most fortunate of those to embark was Father Frank Browne, a theology student in Dublin. On 4 April 1912, he received an unexpected present from his uncle, the Bishop of Cloyne: a first-class ticket for the initial two stops on *Titanic*'s maiden voyage, from Southampton to Cherbourg to Queenstown,

BELOW ANOTHER PHOTOGRAPH TAKEN BY FATHER BROWNE SHOWS AN AMERICAN MEDICAL OFFICIAL INSPECTING PASSENGERS' EYES BEFORE ALLOWING THEM ABOARD. NO ONE SUFFERING FROM TRACHOMA WAS PERMITTED TO TRAVEL TO THE US.

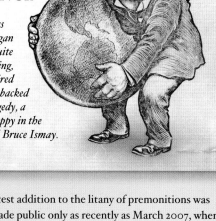

JOHN PIERPONT MORGAN – SURVIVOR

Perhaps the most mysterious cancellation for Titanic *was made by none other than J P Morgan. At one point Morgan was scheduled to occupy the glamorous port promenade suite on B Deck. However, he cancelled his reservation, claiming, according to some sources, that his business interests required him to remain in Europe. Others indicated that Morgan backed out owing to ill health. However, two days after the tragedy, a reporter found him in a French spa town, healthy and happy in the company of his mistress. The suite was taken instead by J Bruce Ismay.*

Ireland. While aboard, Browne was befriended by a wealthy American, who offered to pay his passage to New York. When Browne asked his Jesuit superiors for permission, he received the no-nonsense reply: "Get off that ship." Browne followed his concerned supervisor's instruction, and within just a few days found that the numerous photographs he had taken aboard *Titanic* became famous as the last ones of the doomed ship.

Others with apprehensive relatives or friends were not so fortunate. John Hume, the Scottish violinist who was one of *Titanic*'s eight-man orchestra, had been aboard *Olympic* during the collision with HMS *Hawke*. This had unnerved his mother terribly, and she begged her 28-year-old son not to sail on *Titanic* after a dream told her of terrible consequences. Such a decision could have made gaining future employment with White Star difficult, so Hume boarded with the other musicians at Southampton – and all of them lost their lives. Similarly, Broadway producer Henry B Harris ignored the impassioned pleas of his business associate William Klein not to sail on *Titanic*, and he and his wife embarked in Southampton. Four days later, Mrs Harris was able to enter a lifeboat, but her husband paid the ultimate price.

There were numerous other confirmed instances of foreboding about a tragedy, which were or were not heeded by those scheduled to board. The latest addition to the litany of premonitions was made public only as recently as March 2007, when it was revealed that Alfred Rowe, a Liverpudlian businessman who also owned a ranch in Texas, posted a letter to his wife from Queenstown. Citing the near-collision with *New York* (see page 24) during the departure from Southampton, he told her that *Titanic* was too large, that she was a "positive danger", and that, were he still able to change, he would rather be on *Mauretania* or *Lusitania*. Rowe died in the disaster.

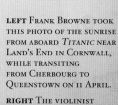

LEFT FRANK BROWNE TOOK THIS PHOTO OF THE SUNRISE FROM ABOARD *TITANIC* NEAR LAND'S END IN CORNWALL, WHILE TRANSITING FROM CHERBOURG TO QUEENSTOWN ON 11 APRIL.

RIGHT THE VIOLINIST JOHN HUME, FROM DUMFRIES, SCOTLAND, FELT UNABLE TO ACCEDE TO HIS MOTHER'S REQUEST NOT TO SAIL ON *TITANIC*. HE WENT DOWN WITH THE SHIP.

THREE DEPARTURES

Wednesday, 10 April dawned fair and breezy. Throughout Southampton, hundreds of crew headed for Berth 44 at the dockyard, where at 6am they were directed to their quarters aboard *Titanic* prior to general muster. Three and a half hours later, another massive influx occurred as most of the second- and third-class passengers arrived on the boat train from Waterloo Station, and were then guided to their separate entrances to the ship. At 11:30am, scarcely half an hour before departure, another train arrived, this time holding first-class passengers, who were efficiently escorted to their staterooms. Promptly at noon, with hundreds of family members, well-wishers and spectators waving and cheering from the quayside, three loud blasts announced departure. The sound had hardly stopped reverberating through the air before disaster nearly struck.

Having been pulled out of the enclosed dock area by five tugs, *Titanic* began to move slowly – and then more rapidly – along the River Test. The turbulence caused by the forward motion of a ship with such incredible size and draft was dissipated harmlessly into the river on her starboard side. But on her port side, the displaced water was trapped between the monstrous ship and the dock's bulkheads. Tied in tandem at Berth 38 were two liners, *Oceanic* and *New York*, that were out of service until they could be coaled.

As *Titanic* swept near them, the displaced water caused *New York* to bounce up and down with such violence that all six of her mooring lines snapped. And as *Titanic* continued, the waves in her wake drew the stern of the now-free *New York* in an arc towards her. George Bowyer, the pilot, immediately ordered "stop engines" and then "full astern", but a

RIGHT Frank Browne caught passengers peering out of the windows when it appeared that the suddenly free *New York* (on right) would collide with *Titanic*.

ABOVE Passengers excitedly boarding *Titanic* in Southampton, while crew below oversee the embarkation. Many considered it a chance of a lifetime to sail on such a ship.

BELOW The special train for *Titanic* passengers – the first and last, it turned out – waiting to depart Waterloo Station, London, on the morning of 10 April.

ABOVE Escorted by tugs, *Titanic* finally gets out into the River Test. Already some aboard were disturbed by what they considered evil omens.

RIGHT Members of the crew in life jackets. Those who had missed the ship were considered lucky.

THE CREWMEN WHO MISSED THE SHIP

Most of the crew of Titanic *signed on during Saturday, 6 April. But when the ship sank, 24 of the original crew were not aboard. Of those, ten were listed as "failed to join", eight as deserted and the others as "left by consent", discharged, transferred or "left ship sick". Among the fortunate were the Slade brothers from Southampton – Bertram, Tom and Alfred – each of whom had been signed on as a fireman. They temporarily left the ship for a pint of beer and missed catching it by moments after they were delayed by a slow train in their path.*

THOMAS HART: DEAD OR ALIVE?

Among the crew officially lost on Titanic *was a fireman whose discharge book named him as Thomas Hart of 51 College Street, Southampton. So one can imagine his mother's shock when, a month later, her son showed up at the door. It turned out that he had never boarded the ship because the night before joining, he had lost his discharge book in a pub. He was then afraid to admit his story immediately after the disaster. No one has ever determined who signed on in Hart's name – and died for his deception.*

collision seemed inevitable. Fortunately, the alert Captain Gale of the tug *Vulcan* swung behind *New York*'s stern and got a wire rope on her port quarter to slow her drift. Danger was averted by no more than a metre or so, and those who had felt ill at ease about coming on the ship must have seen it as another harbinger of bad tidings.

Titanic was now forced to wait an hour while *New York* was taken out of harm's way and additional lines were placed on *Oceanic*. She therefore did not arrive at her first port of call, Cherbourg, until 6:35pm. Cherbourg's piers were not large enough to accommodate *Titanic*, and the two purpose-built White Star tenders, *Nomadic* and *Traffic*, ferried arriving and departing passengers and cargo from ship to harbour. Twenty-two passengers disembarked, to be replaced by 274, each of whom had made the six-hour train ride from Paris aboard the *Train Transatlantique*. Among these were 47-year-old American mining magnate Benjamin Guggenheim; famed English dress designer Lucy, Lady Duff Gordon and her husband, Sir Cosmo; and Denver socialite Mrs James Brown, known to her friends as "Molly".

An hour and a half later, *Titanic* departed for Queenstown, Ireland, where, at 11am on 11 April, she anchored 3.2 kilometres (two miles) offshore, as once again she was too vast to enter the harbour. White Star tenders took off eight passengers – including Frank Browne, whose photographs were the last of the ship – and ferried 120 passengers and 1,385 sacks of mail to the ship. Meanwhile, fireman

ABOVE Titanic *steams towards Cherbourg, her first port of call on her maiden voyage. Fully lit up at night, she made a marvellous sight.*

John Coffee stowed away in the offgoing post and disappeared into his native Queenstown. Onboard, an unknown fireman disturbed passengers when his soot-covered face was seen coming out of the hindmost of the ship's four funnels. It was the dummy funnel used as a ventilator rather than a chimney, as the prankster knew full well, but to some of the squeamish aboard, it was an evil omen.

All was now ready for the transatlantic voyage to New York, so at 1:30pm the American flag was raised and those aboard watched the green of Ireland fade into the distance. For many of them, it was the last time they would ever see land.

BACKGROUND TOP
Titanic at Queenstown. Coincidentally, three years later, Cunard's *Lusitania* was not far from Queenstown when she was sunk by a German U-boat.

BACKGROUND BOTTOM
A first-class cabin passenger's contract ticket for travelling from Southampton to New York, dated 10 April 1912. It cost £26.

BELOW The White Star Line tenders *Ireland* and *America* at Queenstown's Deepwater Quay fully loaded with arriving passengers going out to the ship.

ENCLOSURES
1 The Certificate of Clearance as an "Emigrant ship" for *Titanic* to depart from Southampton. Note that it is dated 11 April.
2 A postcard sent from Queenstown by Escott Robert Phillips, a second-class passenger, to his friend Bill Squires. Phillips was lost when the ship sank, but his 21-year-old daughter Alice escaped in Lifeboat 12.

Ice Ahead

For three days after leaving Queenstown, *Titanic* raced across the Atlantic, accompanied by conditions most passengers loved – blue skies, light winds and calm seas. Yet that state of affairs belied the fact that almost all vessels in the North Atlantic shipping lanes were facing problems of a serious nature. In the far north, the winter had been the mildest in three decades, causing many more icebergs than normal to calve off the Greenland ice shelves. A little farther south, however, temperatures had been cold enough so that as the vast fields of ice drifted south, they did not melt as quickly as usual. The result, as shown by reports of ships during the week beginning 7 April, was that an immense band of ice, extending from 46°North to near 41°30'North and from about 46°18' to 40°40'West, was moving slowly southwest. Since *Titanic* was heading towards "the corner" – a point at 42°North, 47°West at which ships usually set a new course, depending on whether they were going to New York, Boston or other locations – she was aiming directly for this ice.

ABOVE AND BACKGROUND A French pilot chart showing the intended voyage of *Titanic* across the Atlantic Ocean. Most of the cruise went just as planned. but not all.

BELOW Passengers stroll around the second-class boat deck while at anchor off Queenstown, unaware of the terrible conditions they were sailing into.

Second Officer Charles Lightoller

One of the key figures in the chaotic last hours of Titanic *was 38-year-old Second Officer Charles Lightoller, who had also commanded the last four-hour watch (6–10pm) prior to the collision. Lightoller had gone to sea at 13, joined White Star Line in 1900 and been promoted to first officer before being temporarily dropped back to second officer when Chief Officer Henry Wilde joined* Titanic *late. Throughout the evening, Lightoller expressed concerns about the falling temperature and urged his lookouts to keep their eyes peeled for icebergs despite a calm sea that made spotting them exceptionally difficult.*

Sunday was normally a special day aboard ship, and the morning of 14 April was like most others, with Captain Smith conducting the Church of England service in the first-class dining saloon, the assistant purser leading another in the second-class saloon and Father Thomas Byles overseeing the Catholic Mass, first in the second-class lounge, then in the third-class areas. But in the wireless room, the domain of Marconi senior wireless operator Jack Phillips and junior operator Harold Bride, a series of messages began to come through that would soon take on unimagined significance.

In the preceding days, at least a dozen messages had arrived from other ships informing *Titanic* of icebergs ahead. At 9am on the 14th, Phillips received another, from Cunard's *Caronia*, reporting icebergs, "growlers" (smaller but still dangerous pieces of ice) and an extensive field of ice at 42°North, 49–51°West. Phillips immediately took it to Captain Smith, who had it posted on the bridge for his officers. Ice warnings continued to arrive, including some from the Dutch *Noordam* at 11:40am and then, at 1:42pm, from the Greek steamship *Athinai* via White Star's *Baltic*, a message that, rather than post on the bridge, Smith strangely handed to Ismay, who put it in his pocket. Almost simultaneously, another report of ice – at 41°27'North, 50°8'West – was received by Phillips from the German ship *Amerika*, but the chief wireless man, according to Bride, failed to notify any officers.

All told, seven ice warnings were received during the day. One, at 7:30pm, came from the Leyland ship *Californian*, which reported three large icebergs a short distance north of *Titanic*'s route. Bride took it to the bridge, but the message did not reach the captain because he was in the à la carte restaurant at a dinner party given in his honour by the wealthy George and Eleanor Widener of Philadelphia. Yet another message, which confirmed heavy pack ice and icebergs, came at 9:40pm from *Mesaba*, but because Bride was sleeping, Phillips was unable to leave his post to take it to the bridge. Meanwhile, the temperature outside began to drop rapidly, decreasing from 6.1°C (43°F) at 7pm to 0.5°C (33°F) two hours later.

The final ice warning – as it turned out, *Titanic*'s last chance – was sent out at 11pm by Cyril Evans of *Californian*. But the message was not taken by Phillips, who was busy sending and receiving passengers' messages via the Cape Race station in Newfoundland, a task normally carried out at night, when the wireless transmitting range trebled from 650 kilometres (400 miles) during the day to 1,950 kilometres (1,200 miles) at night. Thus, for a variety of reasons, only one of the messages had reached both the captain and the bridge in a timely fashion. In a time of desperate danger, the officers on watch were unaware of the extent of the peril into which they were steaming.

CALIFORNIAN ON THE AIR

As well as monitoring traffic for general messages and specific warnings, wireless officers sent and received messages for passengers. At 11pm on 14 April, Jack Phillips was in contact with Cape Race station, when a message burst in from a nearby ship. "Say, old man, we are stopped and surrounded by ice", transmitted Cyril Evans from Californian. But before Evans could give his location, Phillips heatedly responded, "Shut up! Shut up! I am busy. I am working Cape Race." Evans, hoping to pass on important information, monitored Titanic for 25 minutes, but since Phillips continued to transmit, he finally shut down and went to bed.

The Collision

Despite the repeated warnings of ice throughout the day, by 11:30pm on 14 April, *Titanic* was still racing along at nearly 22½ knots. The ship was well supplied with specialist lookouts, and in such clear conditions, Captain Smith assumed any ice would be seen far ahead. However, not only was the night moonless, thereby eliminating the sheen off the surface of any ice, but the conditions were so calm, with no waves and no breeze, that normal wave action, which would form a lighter ring around the base of any icebergs, was absent.

About 15 metres (50 feet) above the forecastle deck, lookouts Fred Fleet and Reginald Lee stared out of the crow's nest into the darkness. At 11:30pm they spied a misty haze on the horizon but could not make out anything definite, in part because the binoculars for the lookouts had disappeared before the ship reached Queenstown. They could only strain with the naked eye to see through the darkness.

Suddenly, at 11:40pm, Fleet spotted a dark object dead ahead. He immediately rang the 41-centimetre (16-inch) brass bell that hung above him and picked up the phone to the bridge, which was answered by Sixth Officer James Moody. "Iceberg right ahead", Fleet stated. Within moments, First Officer William Murdoch ordered "Hard a-starboard" (dictating that the ship's bow would swing to port), telegraphed the engine room "Stop. Full speed astern" and closed the ship's watertight doors.

BELOW BINOCULARS FROM *TITANIC*. THESE HAVE TOURED THE WORLD AS SOME OF THE MOST INTERESTING ARTEFACTS FROM THE SUNKEN SHIP, AND WERE ON DISPLAY IN LOS ANGELES WHEN THIS PHOTOGRAPH WAS TAKEN.

BELOW ALTHOUGH THIS PICTURE WAS TAKEN HOURS LATER, AFTER THE SUN ROSE, THIS IS THOUGHT TO BE THE ICEBERG WITH WHICH *TITANIC* COLLIDED. SOME PASSENGERS CLAIMED THEY SAW STREAKS OF PAINT ON IT.

ABOVE FIRST OFFICER WILLIAM MURDOCH, WHO DID NOT SURVIVE THE TRAGEDY. ALTHOUGH HE HAS BEEN PORTRAYED NEGATIVELY AT TIMES, THERE IS NO EVIDENCE THAT HIS BEHAVIOUR WAS ANYTHING BUT PROPER THROUGHOUT THE EVENTS.

BELOW THIS PHOTO OF AN ICEBERG WAS THE MAIN FEATURE OF PAGE ONE OF *THE ILLUSTRATED LONDON NEWS* ON 20 APRIL 1912, WHEN THE WEEKLY PAPER CARRIED THE STORY OF THE SINKING OF *TITANIC*.

North Atlantic Icebergs

It is likely that the iceberg with which Titanic *collided calved from a major glacier in West Greenland. Each year, some 10,000–15,000 large icebergs or smaller chunks of ice known as "growlers" float south to the region in which* Titanic *sank. Icebergs are composed of fresh water, with approximately seven-eighths of their mass below the water line; mass does not refer to height out of the water, which can vary greatly in proportion. The iceberg that* Titanic *hit was estimated to be 15–30 metres (50–100 feet) high above the water and 60–120 metres (200–400 feet) long.*

ENCLOSURES
This tragic series of three telegrams shows the desperate correspondence between *Titanic* and *Olympic*.

BACKGROUND THE SECOND-CLASS DINNER MENU FOR THE NIGHT OF THE COLLISION.

Titanic began to swing to port away from the iceberg – one point, then two – but it was not enough. The iceberg had been spotted at less than 450 metres (500 yards), and although the top of the ship did not collide with it, deep below the waterline some 90 metres (300 feet) of the hull scraped and bumped against the ice. The intense pressure caused the plates to buckle and the rivets to pop, opening a long, intermittent gash that penetrated the first five compartments, including the forward boiler room.

Within a minute, Captain Smith had raced to the bridge, and he quickly sent Fourth Officer Joseph Boxhall to ascertain the extent of the damage. Most of the passengers were not aware of the severity of the impact, although some were intrigued that large fragments of ice had come cascading down on the forward well deck, while others claimed to have felt anything from a slight shock or trembling to a strong jar accompanied by a grinding noise.

It was considerably worse than that in boiler room No. 6, where Second Engineer James Hesketh and Frederick Barrett, a leading stoker, heard a terrible rending sound and water suddenly exploded through a gash about 60 centimetres (2 feet) above the floor. They dived into the next room as the watertight door closed, only to find another tear in the steel plates and another jet of water shooting towards them. By the time they climbed to a higher deck, the water in No. 6 boiler room had already risen 2.4 metres (8 feet).

Within 15 minutes, Boxhall reported back to Captain Smith, who shortly thereafter received an even grimmer report from Thomas Andrews of Harland & Wolff. Andrews had quickly realized the gravity of the situation. *Titanic* could float with any two of her watertight compartments flooded; she could even remain afloat if it were the first four compartments that were breached. But five had been opened up, and the fifth – boiler room No. 6 – and those after it did not have watertight bulkheads that extended to the uppermost decks. When boiler room No. 6 finished flooding, the water still pouring in would reach E deck, and would then overflow into the sixth "watertight" compartment from above. As each successive compartment filled and the bow was pulled further under, the next compartment would again start to fill.

Andrews informed Smith that the "unsinkable" ship was going to do just that. No one knew better than Andrews that they were far short of the necessary lifeboats, meaning many of the passengers, like *Titanic* herself, had only an hour or two to live.

RIGHT This evocative picture from France's *Le Petit Journal* does not show the way *Titanic* actually struck the iceberg, but it got its message across to its readers.

BACKGROUND The top of the front page of *The Illustrated London News* when the loss of *Titanic* was reported.

ABOVE This photo of a mother and child being given assistance was taken by Frank Browne. It shows the extensive riveting on the massive plates on the sides of *Titanic*.

THOMAS ANDREWS

No one knew Titanic *better than 39-year-old Thomas Andrews, managing director for Harland & Wolff in charge of design. Andrews joined the company at the age of 16 as an apprentice and eventually rose to a position of prominence. He boarded* Titanic *in Belfast to determine if any adjustments were needed, and to oversee the company's "Guarantee Group" that would effect the changes. After advising Captain Smith that the ship was doomed, he encouraged passengers to make their way to the lifeboats. He was last seen in the first-class smoking room, staring into space with his life-jacket in front of him.*

Man the Lifeboats

As soon as it became obvious that *Titanic* was mortally wounded, Captain Smith ordered the crew to be mustered, the lifeboats to be uncovered and the passengers brought up to the decks. He then directed Fourth Officer Joseph Boxhall to calculate the ship's position. His estimate – 41°46'North, 50°14'West, which was off by many miles – was taken to Jack Phillips in the wireless room, who began sending out distress calls.

The inefficiency and confusion brought about by sailing on what was perceived as an "unsinkable" ship quickly became apparent. There was not a consistent plan of action, most of the crew had not received adequate training in launching the lifeboats and the captain had not held the standard passenger lifeboat drill. Moreover, most of the passengers were already in their cabins, there was no public address system and when the stewards informed the

passengers of the situation, they gave widely varying instructions. Slowly, however, a number of people made their way to the promenades and boat decks.

At 12:25am, Smith ordered the loading of lifeboats, with women and children first. Even this was carried out haphazardly as, on port side, men were denied access to the boats, while on starboard they were allowed in if there were no women waiting. The actual loading of the boats began to bring home the reality of the dangers, and many passengers crowded the pursers' offices to demand their valuables back.

Several other problems became apparent as the boats were loaded. First, many of the passengers were extremely hesitant and, after looking at the water far below, chose to not leave the comforts of the ship for the tiny, creaking vessels. In addition, the officers were concerned about loading the boats too heavily, evidently unaware that the new Welin davits were able to withstand the full

RIGHT This, the only known picture of the wireless office aboard *Titanic*, was taken by Father Browne on his short stay aboard the ship. Jack Phillips spent his last hours desperately signalling for help from here.

BACKGROUND The lifeboats of *Titanic*. Not only were there not enough, but many of the crew did not know how to deal effectively with them and most were sent out only partially full.

BELOW This well known painting shows the bravery, the anguish and the fear shown by passengers and crew alike as the women and children were loaded into the lifeboats.

CQD: the Wireless Efforts

At 12:15am, Jack Phillips started tapping out the emergency signal "CQD" (often said to stand for "Come Quick, Danger"), followed by Titanic's call letters – MGY – and her estimated position. Ten minutes later, Harold Cottam of Carpathia, 94 kilometres (58 miles) away, came onto the frequency to tell Phillips there were numerous messages from Cape Cod for Titanic. *Receiving Phillips' distress signal, the amazed Cottam responded, "Shall I tell my captain? Do you require assistance?" "Yes", Phillips replied. "Come quick." Cottam raced to the bridge, Captain Arthur Rostron was awoken, and within minutes* Carpathia *was on her way.*

RIGHT The life-jacket worn by Madeleine Astor. It is now part of the *Titanic* Historical Society Collection held at the *Titanic* Museum in Indian Orchard, Massachusetts.

load of 65 adults. One plan was to lower the boats half-full, and then take more passengers from the gangway doors at water level, but the men sent to open the doors disappeared. Boat after boat went down the side with numerous empty spaces on it.

At about 12:45am, First Officer William Murdoch ordered the first lifeboat – Number 7 on the starboard side – to be lowered away with only 28 people aboard. Near the same time, Boxhall fired off the first of a series of distress rockets. Hope increased when the lights of another ship became visible some 10–16 kilometres (6–10 miles) off the port side.

Lifeboat 5 was the second boat lowered, with some 40 occupants. In command of it was Third Officer Herbert Pittman, whom Murdoch sent so that he could also look after the other boats when they reached the water. Also in the boat was Quartermaster Alfred Olliver, who, as it descended, desperately tried to find the plug for the hole through which excess water drained when the boat was stored. Confronted by uncooperative passengers, he succeeded in finding and inserting the plug only

after the boat had reached the sea and started taking water.

Meanwhile, on the port side, some 25 women were loaded into Lifeboat 6, with Quartermaster Robert Hichens and lookout Frederick Fleet, who had first seen the iceberg, as the only crew. Second Officer Charles Lightoller ordered Hichens to row the vessel to the ship in the distance and come back for more passengers. As the boat started to descend, Mrs Margaret "Molly" Brown of Denver – who had just persuaded several fearful women to get in and was going to help out elsewhere – was grabbed by two well-meaning acquaintances and dropped 1.2 metres (four feet) over the side into the boat. She quickly realized there were not enough men to row to the distant light and demanded more. With Lightoller's blessing, Major Arthur Peuchen, a Canadian yachtsman, swung out 1.8 metres (6 feet) onto the ropes and let himself down hand-over-hand.

As more boats reached the water below, the anxious people still aboard *Titanic* began to realize that many of them were not going to survive.

LEFT Major Arthur Peuchen, the yachtsman who volunteered to help row Lifeboat 6. He survived, but suffered the stigma of having been a man in one of the lifeboats for the rest of his life.

RIGHT An illustration of a lifeboat being lowered down the side of *Titanic* shows how far the boats had to descend to the water and why some passengers were concerned about entering them.

LEFT A low-level view of the lifeboats aboard *Titanic*, as the dogs aboard would have seen them. The dogs were less fortunate regarding the lifeboats than even the human passengers were.

Dog the Lifeboats

Just as every other whim of Titanic's *first-class passengers was catered to, dog owners were pleased by spotless kennels and crew detailed to walk the dogs daily. There were so many dogs aboard that a show had even been scheduled. Although honeymooning Helen Bishop had insisted her dog Frou Frou reside in her cabin, she left it behind because she acknowledged there was not enough room for all the people. Two dogs did survive, however. Margaret Hays took her Pomeranian into Lifeboat 7, and Henry Harper escaped in Lifeboat 3 with his Pekinese named Sun Yat Sen.*

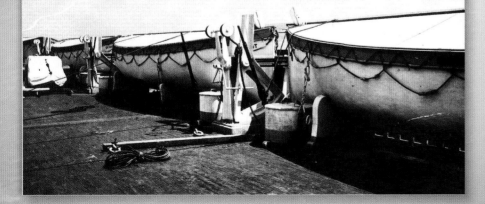

THE BAND PLAYS ON

While *Titanic*'s bows dipped deeper into the water, and the lifeboat operation proceeded, passengers and crew responded to the emergency in many different ways. Some passengers steadfastly remained in their cabins, refusing to believe there was an emergency. Others, such as 21-year-old tennis star R Norris Williams – who was travelling to the US prior to entering Harvard – stoically wandered the ship, unwilling to enter a lifeboat when women and children were still aboard. At one point, Norris and his father found a steward unable to open the door to a first-class cabin, in which a woman was beginning to panic. Williams dropped his shoulder and broke the door in, prompting the steward to announce that he would have to report him for damaging company property.

Upstairs, several members of Wallace Hartley's eight-man orchestra began playing in the first-class lounge to help relieve the tension. The other

BELOW RICHARD NORRIS WILLIAMS WENT ON TO BECOME ONE OF THE WORLD'S PREMIER TENNIS PLAYERS AND REPRESENTED THE UNITED STATES IN DAVIS CUP ACTION NUMEROUS TIMES, INCLUDING AS CAPTAIN.

members soon joined them and eventually, as the passengers headed outside, the band followed them to the boat deck. Legend has it that the bandsmen remained at their instruments until the very end. Whether true or not, they certainly continued to play even after hope of rescue was gone, and they made the horribly anxious final hours of many people considerably calmer.

Meanwhile, members of the crew desperately struggled to minimize the disaster. Fourth Officer Joseph Boxhall was joined by Quartermaster George Rowe in firing off distress rockets at five-minute intervals. By means of a Morse lamp, they also tried to contact the unknown ship, which was so close that they could make out her red and green sidelights. Despite their best efforts, after about an hour the mysterious ship vanished into the night. Throughout the same period, all 34 engineering officers remained at their posts, maintaining *Titanic*'s lighting and other electrical systems until moments before she sank; every one of them was lost with the ship.

Many passengers also showed remarkable courage in the crisis, and did their utmost to help others. Four men – railway director Charles M Hays, automobile designer Washington Augustus Roebling II, Howard Case and Thornton Davidson – turned down the opportunity to enter Lifeboat 3 and instead assisted numerous women and children at a variety of boat stations before calmly

ABOVE SEVEN OF THE EIGHT MEMBERS OF *TITANIC*'S ORCHESTRA. FROM LEFT: FRED CLARKE, PERCY TAYLOR, THEODORE BRAILEY, LEADER WALLACE HARTLEY, GEORGES KRINS, JOHN HUME AND JOHN WOODWARD. NOT PICTURED: CELLIST ROGER BRICOUX.

BELOW LIFEBOAT 15 THREATENS TO CRUSH LIFEBOAT 13 FROM ABOVE. HAD THE BOAT ON THE WATER NOT JUST ESCAPED, ANOTHER 64 PEOPLE WOULD UNDOUBTEDLY HAVE LOST THEIR LIVES.

BACKGROUND MUSIC SHEETS OF "NEARER MY GOD TO THEE" IN FRENCH (LEFT PAGE) AND ENGLISH (RIGHT PAGE). THE HYMN IS OFTEN SAID TO BE THE LAST SONG PLAYED ABOARD *TITANIC*.

DANGER FROM ABOVE

Shortly before 1:30am, Lifeboat 13 was lowered with 64 people, swaying dangerously as it descended. When it reached the surface, water pouring from the flooded condenser exhaust system pushed it directly beneath Lifeboat 15. The crew tried to release the ropes, but they were so taut the mechanism would not work. The cries of those on Lifeboat 13 were not heard, and Lifeboat 15 continued down until those below could touch its hull. Finally, two crewmen, Fred Barrett and Robert Hopkins, grabbed knives and cut the ropes, narrowly preventing the boat being crushed.

accepting their fates. Others seemed unconcerned, perhaps because of their fervent belief in *Titanic* being unsinkable. For example, after hearing the call to don life-jackets, Major Archibald Butt, military aide to President William Howard Taft, finished his card game in the first-class smoking room with Clarence Moore, Harry Widener and William Carter before adjourning to see what was happening. Colonel Archibald Gracie, an American historian, cancelled his Monday morning match with the ship's squash professional before making his way to the boat deck.

All the while, lifeboats continued to be loaded haphazardly. At about 1:00am, number 3 went down the side with fewer than 50 people, 15 of them crew. Shortly thereafter, First Officer William Murdoch prepared the first of the two smaller lifeboats, with a capacity of 40. With only a handful of people nearby, rather than call for others, Murdoch had it launched holding only a dozen: five passengers – including Sir Cosmo Duff Gordon and his wife, Lucile – and seven crew.

As the deck of the ship tilted more precariously and the true danger of the situation became increasingly obvious, the officers finally began to load the boats

more fully. Around 1:20am, Lifeboat 9 was sent out with 56 people. About 20 minutes later, numbers 11 and 15 had about 70 occupants each – more than the tested limit. As Lifeboat 14 was lowered at 1:30am containing some 60 people (almost all women), Fifth Officer Harold Lowe went with it in order to take charge of the boats on the water. But he was so worried they would be overwhelmed by frightened men that he pulled his revolver to keep them back.

The boats were running out, and so was time for those aboard *Titanic*.

ABOVE THE SIGNAL LAMPS BEING INSPECTED BY A PORT OFFICIAL WHILE *TITANIC* WAS AT QUEENSTOWN. TRAGICALLY, THE "MYSTERY SHIP" DID NOT RESPOND TO REQUESTS FOR EMERGENCY HELP VIA THE LAMPS.

BOTTOM FAR LEFT THE FUNERAL FOR WALLACE HARTLEY ON 25 MAY 1912 IN HIS HOMETOWN OF COLNE, LANCASHIRE, DREW THOUSANDS FROM ALL OVER THE COUNTRY WISHING TO PAY THEIR LAST RESPECTS.

LEFT A MEMORIAL TO THE MUSICIANS ABOARD *TITANIC*. THIS WAS ERECTED IN SOUTHAMPTON IN 1990 ON THE SAME SITE AS ONE UNVEILED IN 1913 BUT DESTROYED DURING THE SECOND WORLD WAR.

THE FINAL NUMBER

There has long been debate over the last music played by Titanic's *bandsmen. Major Peuchen claimed he heard "Alexander's Ragtime Band" while in Lifeboat 6. Wireless operator Harold Bride stated that after playing ragtime tunes, the band concluded with the hymn "Autumn". This was not in White Star's music book, however, and it has been suggested that Bride was actually referring to the waltz "Songe d'Automne". Or was it, as numerous survivors claimed, "Nearer My God to Thee"? This was Wallace Hartley's favourite hymn, but it still leaves open the question of which of three tunes the hymn was played to: "Bethany", "Horbury" or "Proprior Deo".*

The Rich, Famous and Unfortunate

Since *Titanic* was considered the most luxurious ship in the world, it is not surprising that some of those who died essentially comprised a "who's who'" of the financial, social and artistic worlds.

The wealthiest person aboard was 47-year-old John Jacob Astor IV. The great-grandson and namesake of a man who had earned both fame and enormous fortune first in the fur trade and then in real estate investments in New York City, Astor had taken over the management of his family's New York properties while still in his mid-twenties. He made large sums from owning overcrowded and run-down tenements that were rented to immigrants, but he also profited from building offices, apartment buildings and hotels. In 1897, he financed the Astoria Hotel adjoining his cousin's Waldorf Hotel, and the new complex

BELOW The original Waldorf-Astoria complex. The Waldorf Hotel opened in 1893 and the Astoria Hotel four years later. Today, this site is occupied by the Empire State Building.

became world-famous as the Waldorf-Astoria. Astor also wrote science fiction, invented mechanical devices and served in the military long enough to reach the rank of colonel.

Another prominent military figure aboard *Titanic* was Major Archibald Butt. He was originally a journalist, through which he gained many contacts in Washington, leading in turn to him being appointed as first secretary of the American Embassy in Mexico. In 1898, during the Spanish–American War, he joined the army as a lieutenant. In the next eight years, he served in the Philippines and Cuba before becoming a military aid to President Theodore Roosevelt and then to his successor, William Howard Taft. Suffering ill health in early 1912, Butt holidayed in Europe for six weeks – travelling for part of it with the artist Francis Millet – before the two boarded *Titanic*.

Like Astor, 50-year-old George Widener came from a wealthy background. His father had been a founding partner of the hugely successful Philadelphia Traction Company and was on the board of Fidelity Trust, the bank that controlled IMMC, owner of the White Star Line. The younger Widener eventually took charge of the Philadelphia Traction Company and oversaw the development of lucrative cable and electric streetcar operations. A patron of the arts, he lived at Lynnewood Hall, a 110-room French classical-style mansion outside Philadelphia. Although Widener's wife, Eleanor, survived, Widener and their 27-year-old son, Harry, did not.

Like Madeleine Astor and Eleanor Widener, Pennsylvania steel millionaire Arthur Ryerson's wife Emily boarded Lifeboat 4, and like the

LEFT Major Archibald Butt began his career in journalism as a reporter for the *Louisville Courier-Journal*. While an officer in the US Army, he served in the Philippines and Cuba.

RIGHT John Jacob Astor and his wife Madeleine. She escaped in Lifeboat 4 and in August gave birth to John Jacob Astor V. She relinquished any claim to the Astor fortune when she married William Dick in 1916.

Astor at the Disaster

In 1909, Astor divorced his wife of 18 years, and two years later he married Madeleine Force, who, at 18, was two years younger than his son. Gossip about the respectability of the union led the couple to spend the winter abroad, hoping the scandal would die down in their absence. They joined Titanic *at Cherbourg. On the night of the disaster, Astor helped Madeleine, who was five months pregnant, into Lifeboat 4 and then asked to accompany her. After being told that only women and children would be admitted, he calmly stepped back and waved goodbye.*

LEFT Isidor and Ida Straus. In the years immediately following the disaster, their decision to stay with each other aboard made them perhaps the most revered of all *Titanic* passengers.

He also had once been elected to Congress. Now, after the collision, Ida started to get into Lifeboat 8, but she changed her mind and returned to her husband. Others nearby appealed to Straus to enter the boat, stating that no one would mind him doing so, but he refused as long as there were women and children aboard. The couple left the deck to share their final moments, while the lifeboat was sent out less than half-full.

Throughout the night, other influential men – including Charles M Hayes, the president of Canada's Grand Trunk Pacific Railroad, American short-story writer Jacques Futrelle and Christopher Head, a former mayor of Chelsea – showed remarkable poise. Few displayed more panache, however, than American mining magnate Benjamin Guggenheim. When the futility of the situation became apparent, he and his valet Victor Giglio disappeared below. Returning in full evening dress, Guggenheim announced: "We've dressed up in our best and are prepared to go down like gentlemen."

others, she lost her husband. The Ryersons had been visiting Europe when they learned of the accidental death of their son, Arthur Jr. Wishing to hurry home, they booked passage on *Titanic*. Unbeknown to them, a distant cousin, William E Ryerson, was also aboard as a dining saloon steward; he survived the tragedy.

Meanwhile, Ida Straus, the wife of another wealthy passenger, was unwilling to leave her husband. Isidor Straus had emigrated with his family from Bavaria at the age of nine in 1854, and through years of work had built a mercantile empire, eventually acquiring ownership with his brother of Macy's department store in New York.

THE SAGA OF LIFEBOAT 4

One of the first lifeboats to be readied was Lifeboat 4, which at 12:30am was swung out and lowered one level so that it was next to the promenade deck. There, a group of well-heeled passengers – the Astors, Wideners, Ryersons, Thayers and Carters – had been assembled. However, no one could open the windows in the canopy surrounding the deck, and after half an hour the group was shuttled up to the boat deck. But now there was no one to haul the lifeboat back up again, so, after another lengthy wait, they once again traipsed down to the promenade deck. There the windows were finally opened, and the women and children were able to enter the lifeboat. Despite there being only about 35 people in the boat, husbands were not allowed to enter it, and at about 1:55am it was finally lowered, one of the last boats to leave the ship.

The Ship Sinks

As the front end of the ship sank deeper, among the last hopes for survival were the four collapsible boats. These had canvas sides that could be raised and held up by stanchions, but on a normal basis could be stored flat. Collapsible C was loaded to two-thirds capacity before a group of men appeared ready to rush it around 1:45am. Chief Purser Herbert McElroy stopped them by firing his revolver twice. Just as it began to be lowered, two other men quietly sneaked into it. They were William Carter, who had been refused entry into Lifeboat 4 with his family, and J Bruce Ismay of White Star.

At 2:05am, Collapsible D was the last boat launched, when Chief Officer Henry Wilde sent it out only half-full because, with the water rapidly rising, he believed it might not otherwise get off at all. As it began to be lowered, Second Officer Charles Lightoller drew his pistol and ordered several crewmen to form a barrier to prevent it from being overwhelmed by a surge of men arriving from the lower decks. Wilde instructed Lightoller to get in the boat, but the Second Officer refused to leave his post. Meanwhile, as Collapsible D dropped past them on the promenade deck, two first-class passengers – Hugh Woolmer and Mauritz Björnstrom-Steffansson – seeing the water lapping the deck, leapt together into the boat.

Lightoller was not alone in maintaining his post until the end. Andrew Latimer, a chief steward, gave his own life-jacket to a woman without one, then continued to load passengers into boats until they had all been launched. The five postal clerks hauled sacks of registered mail – many weighing up to 45 kilograms (100 pounds) – up one level after another to keep ahead of the rising water. All five lost their lives, and it is estimated that 3,364 sacks of mail went down with the ship. Similarly, Jack Phillips and Harold Bride remained at their wireless even after Captain Smith told them and other crew members to save themselves.

Meanwhile, *Titanic*'s stern had risen higher out of the water because of the sinking bow, and at about

BELOW AND BACKGROUND THIS DIAGRAM SHOWS THE DIFFERENT DECKS ON *TITANIC*, AND GIVES AN IDEA OF THE COMPLICATED ROUTES THIRD-CLASS PASSENGERS WOULD HAVE HAD TO FOLLOW TO REACH THE BOAT DECK.

ABOVE CHIEF OFFICER HENRY F WILDE HAD THE MISFORTUNE OF BEING TRANSFERRED OVER TO *TITANIC* AT THE LAST MOMENT FROM *OLYMPIC*, JOINING IN SOUTHAMPTON. PREVIOUS CHIEF OFFICER WILLIAM MURDOCH BECAME FIRST OFFICER INSTEAD.

RIGHT A DIAGRAM SHOWING HOW, IN HER FINAL TRAGIC MOMENTS, *TITANIC'S* STERN RAISED OUT OF THE WATER, HER HULL BROKE IN TWO AND SHE SANK BENEATH THE SURFACE.

The Tragedy of Third-Class

Although the legend that third-class passengers were locked below decks is untrue, they still suffered far greater losses than the upper classes. Stewards were not as thorough or prompt in getting third-class passengers to the boat deck, and a lack of familiarity with the layout of the upper decks made escape upwards more difficult. Then, at points, men were prevented access to the boat deck, although women were allowed up. As a result, although roughly 62 per cent of first-class was saved, and almost 59 per cent of second-class, only some 25 per cent of third-class passengers lived to tell the tale.

36

THE FATE OF CAPTAIN SMITH

Captain Smith does not appear to have followed any unified course of action in the final two hours aboard Titanic. He was last seen with certainty near the bridge after 2:00am, having told crew members to save themselves. Several legends sprang up about his final moments. One stated he carried a baby out to one of the boats before swimming back into the maelstrom. Another indicated he reached Collapsible B, but finding it overcrowded, simply swam away. Most likely, however, he remained on the bridge and went down with his ship.

LEFT An illustration from *The Illustrated London News* showing Captain Smith handing a baby to survivors on Collapsible B before returning towards the wreckage. There is no evidence this actually occurred.

BELOW An artist's impression of *Titanic* in her death throes before going to the bottom of the sea. In reality, the night was pitch black, several of her funnels came off, and she split in two.

2:17am, a massive roar was heard by those in the lifeboats as the increasing angle caused all the ship's fittings and furniture suddenly to crash towards the bow. Moments later, the stern approached a 45° angle, maintaining that position for some 30 seconds before the lights finally failed. Then, the two front funnels toppled into the water, throwing out clouds of steam and soot. Finally, with a sound like thunder, the stress on the hull snapped *Titanic* in two between the third and fourth funnels. The bow slid beneath the surface and planed diagonally downwards, while the stern seemed to settle briefly before plunging to the bottom.

Some of those still aboard were sucked to the depths with the ship, while others were simply thrown into the freezing water. Both Collapsibles A and B were washed overboard, with those already loaded into the former swept out of it. Others managed to climb aboard or grab onto its sides in the midst of the chaos, and it remained afloat, although partly flooded.

Collapsible B also saved many lives, although it fell into the water upside down. Lightoller and Colonel Archibald Gracie were sucked under by the force of the sinking ship, both barely reaching the surface again, Lightoller only when thrust up by a blast of air forced from a ventilator. They managed to reach Collapsible B and pull themselves onto the bottom of the upturned boat with some

30 other men, who struggled all night to stay aboard. Also there was Harold Bride, who was trapped in an air pocket under the boat for 45 minutes, then had to hang onto its side before being pulled out of the water by those in Lifeboat 12. Not so fortunate was his colleague Jack Phillips, who reached the boat, but died of exposure during the night. Tragically, the same was true of countless others.

Afloat in the Middle of the Ocean

Where *Titanic* had been so shortly before, the ocean was now dotted only with 20 boats, bits of flotsam and hundreds of individuals in the icy water crying for help. Although far better off than those in the water – most of whom quickly died – the people in the boats still did not know when help would arrive, or if it were on the way at all. Those in the boats were a mixed bag from the broad selection of people aboard the ship, and accordingly behaved in widely different fashions.

BACKGROUND AND MAIN IMAGE BELOW With Quartermaster Robert Hichens standing in the stern, Lifeboat 6 approaches the rescuing *Carpathia*. Hichens' reputation was severely damaged by his behaviour after *Titanic* sank, and in 1914 he moved to South Africa to work as a harbour-master.

No stranger tale unfolded than in Lifeboat 6, where Quartermaster Robert Hichens seemed more concerned with asserting authority than saving lives. When Major Arthur Peuchen let himself down the ropes to join the boat, Hichens quickly assigned him to row, along with lookout Frederick Fleet, while taking the tiller himself. The quartermaster had initially been ordered to take the boat to the mysterious ship in the distance, but before they could do so an officer called for them to come back alongside. Hichens ignored the order, and instead decided to get as far away from *Titanic* as possible before she sank.

Fleet and Peuchen, however, had difficulty propelling the boat alone, and Hichens refused to row, so Margaret Brown grabbed an oar and began rowing herself. She was quickly joined by several other women.

Going Back for Survivors

Although the frantic cries of those in the water disturbed many in the lifeboats, most remained safely at a distance to avoid being swamped by the desperate people. In Lifeboat 8, the Countess of Rothes and three others proposed going back to help, but were overruled. Similarly, in Lifeboat 1, fireman Charles Hendrickson was unable to convince the others. In the initial period after the sinking, only Lifeboat 4, under Walter Perkis, made a serious effort to collect others; seven or eight were rescued, although two of them died that night.

ABOVE The 33-year-old Countess of Rothes not only took the tiller of Lifeboat 8 and helped row, but was one of the most outspoken in favour of going back to save others.

INSERTS BELOW Lifeboats upon the arrival of *Carpathia* hours after *Titanic* sank. Left: one with a sail having been rigged; right: Lifeboat 14 under Fifth Officer Harold Lowe towing Collapsible D.

Throughout the night, even after the mystery ship disappeared and *Titanic* went down, Mrs Brown managed to keep up the spirits of the party, despite the quartermaster displaying an ever-increasing attitude of doom and gloom. When they met Lifeboat 16, in which a stoker was suffering terribly from the cold, "Molly" Brown stood to the fore, wrapping her fur coat around him and likely saved his life.

In Lifeboat 8, the 33-year-old Countess of Rothes had a similar impact, both rowing and taking charge of the tiller. So grateful was Able-bodied Seaman (AB) Thomas Jones for her spirit and labour that he later took the number plate from the boat and gave it to her.

Meanwhile, when Lifeboat 4 finally reached the water, one of the crew called out that they were in need of another man to row. Quartermaster Walter Perkis immediately slid down the ropes and took charge. Despite objections from some of the nervous passengers, he guided the boat towards *Titanic*'s

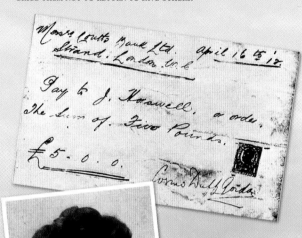

HANGING ON TO COLLAPSIBLE B

Of the survivors, few had a harder night than those on Collapsible B. So many men hauled themselves aboard the overturned boat that it was in constant danger of sinking. To the horror of Archibald Gracie, some then prevented others from climbing on; baker Charles Joughin, for example, was pushed away until someone aboard died, opening a space for him. Eventually, Lightoller organized the men so that they could lean from one side of the boat to the other on his command, keeping the collapsible evenly balanced and helping to avoid foundering.

stern, hoping to pick up more people at the rear companionway. Finding the doors under water, he nevertheless saved two crewmen before moving away from the ship.

One individual who had to wait a good deal longer for help was saloon steward Harold Phillimore. Having jumped from the boat deck in *Titanic*'s final seconds, he clung atop a piece of wreckage with another man until the other slipped into the frigid waters. After about an hour and a half, those aboard Lifeboat 14 under Fifth Officer Harold Lowe – seeking any survivors among the floating bodies – heard Phillimore's calls for help and pulled him into their boat.

One of the most disturbing stories emanated from Lifeboat 1, which had only 12 of its 40 spaces occupied. First, there was friction between lookout George Symons, who was nominally in charge, and first-class passenger Henry Stengel, who wanted to be. Then, as the occupants of the lifeboat watched the ship go down several hundred yards away, the idea was broached about going back to help those in the water. Lucile, Lady Duff Gordon, objected, and Symons refused to order it, so they remained where they were. It later emerged that Sir Cosmo Duff Gordon had offered each of the seven crewmen £5. He insisted this was to help replace their lost kit, but others alleged it was so they would not take the boat to where it could be swamped. True or not, the charge haunted Sir Cosmo for the rest of his life. Meanwhile, another man who would be criticized for his actions that night – J Bruce Ismay – sat silently on Collapsible C, facing away from the ship he had done so much to create.

Rescued

Within moments of receiving the emergency message from *Titanic*, Captain Arthur Rostron ordered his ship, the Cunard liner *Carpathia*, to speed towards the coordinates Jack Phillips had transmitted. Ordering all off-duty firemen and trimmers to the boilers, he drove the ship at a speed she had never before attained, nor ever would again: 17½ knots – three more than what was considered her top rate. Adding extra lookouts, he maintained the pace even when *Carpathia* reached the region dotted with icebergs. At 3:00am, Rostron ordered rockets to be fired at 15-minute intervals, so survivors would know help was on the way. But at about 3:30am, reaching *Titanic*'s supposed position, he could see nothing but open sea, so, grimly, he proceeded on.

Miles to the east, meanwhile, where *Titanic* had actually gone down, Fifth Officer Harold Lowe was also demonstrating admirable presence of mind. After the ship sank, he gathered four lifeboats – 4, 10, 12 and Collapsible D – near his own number 14 and had them lashed together to make a more stable and easily seen mass. He then emptied the passengers from his lifeboat into the others. Lowe hoped to save as many people from the freezing water as possible, but knowing that his boat would be swamped if he went into the midst of the flailing mass, he waited until the cries had subsided. He then searched through the bobbing bodies and eventually picked up four survivors.

To those aboard the small boats in the middle of the icy ocean, the night seemed interminable, and the freezing temperatures threatened anybody still alive. When Collapsible A finally met Lowe's group of boats, the people in it were sitting in several feet of cold water, and as Lowe transferred them to the other boats, he found that three were dead. The minutes continued to tick by, but finally a light could be seen in the distance. *Carpathia* was approaching.

Just after 4:00am, Rostron ordered the engines stopped, and as his men searched the dark waters, a green light was seen 275 metres (300 yards) ahead. It was Lifeboat 2, under the charge of Fourth Officer Joseph Boxhall; at 4:10am, Elizabeth Allen became the first survivor to be taken aboard. Shortly thereafter, Boxhall reported to Rostron that *Titanic* was gone.

ABOVE AND BACKGROUND *Carpathia* was never intended to rival the great luxury liners. Coming into service in 1903, she had vast refrigerated areas to transport various foods, but carried only second- and third-class passengers.

RIGHT Captain Arthur Rostron received many honours. In 1913 he was awarded the Congressional Medal of Honor. He was later knighted and Cunard made him captain of the company flagship, *Mauretania*.

RIGHT A special medal issued to Captain Rostron. It reads: "For heroically saving the seven hundred and four passengers of the Titanic in mid-ocean. The thanks of Congress. July 6, 1912. To Arthur Henry Rostron."

Captain Rostron's Preparations

Captain Rostron knew that every moment Titanic's passengers were left outside might prove fatal. Therefore, as Carpathia steamed forwards, he made detailed rescue preparations. Rostron had the ship's three doctors establish separate medical stations in the dining rooms. Public areas and cabins were stocked with blankets, warm clothing, food and hot drinks. Electric lights were strung over the sides to make boarding easier, and ladders, chair slings, nets and even bags for small children were readied to help or hoist the survivors up. Even the cranes were prepared so they could haul up any luggage or mail that might have been saved.

RIGHT Fifth Officer Harold Lowe proved perhaps the most level-headed of *Titanic*'s senior officers on the night of the tragedy. Sadly, his many life-saving contributions were never appropriately recognized.

FAR RIGHT Although initially considerably underloaded, Collapsible D picked up many more passengers when it joined Fifth Officer Lowe's small armada. Here it makes its way slowly towards *Carpathia*.

BELOW A boatload of survivors – their anxious wait now over – prepare to board *Carpathia*, as one seaman from the rescuing ship looks on from above.

As dawn came, the lifeboats began making their way towards *Carpathia*. Second Office Lightoller, still in charge of the balancing act on upturned Collapsible B, gained the attention of Lifeboat 12, which separated from Lowe's flotilla to pick them up. They then turned to the ship but, being so heavily loaded, made only slow progress. Meanwhile, many people, often too cold and numb to hold on to anything, were lifted by *Carpathia*'s crewmen and brought aboard in slings. It was a painfully slow process, and it was not until 8:10am that Lightoller, having guided Lifeboat 12 to the ship with 75 people in it, became the final person to reach safety.

At 8:30am, *Californian*, which had transmitted the ice warning that Phillips had ignored, became the second ship to arrive. Leaving that vessel, under Captain Stanley Lord, to conduct a thorough search of the area, Rostron steamed west, towards New York. Despite suffering so severely from his lengthy time in the water that he had to be carried off *Carpathia* in New York, *Titanic* wireless officer Harold Bride in the meantime was co-opted to help Harold Cottam in the wireless room. The two worked non-stop sending messages from the survivors, transmitting an official list of the survivors and contacting White Star Line.

Meanwhile, one of *Carparthia*'s scheduled passengers, the artist Colin Campbell Cooper, produced two evocative paintings of the rescue. He and his wife also gave their cabin to three women from *Titanic*. It was a gesture repeated time and again, as those already aboard – who had been sailing for the Mediterranean – did their best to comfort the bereaved, before (for many of the latter) the dreadful ordeal continued ashore.

ABOVE COTTAM AND BRIDE WORKED ALL NIGHT SO THAT *TITANIC* SURVIVORS COULD CONTACT LOVED ONES. THIS TELEGRAM IS FROM EDITH ROSENBAUM AND READS "SAFE *CARPATHIA*, NOTIFY MOTHER".

BOTTOM ALL THAT WAS LEFT OF *TITANIC* WHEN *CARPATHIA* REACHED NEW YORK WAS HER LIFEBOATS, WHICH WERE LEFT AT THE WHITE STAR PIER BEFORE ROSTRON DOCKED HIS SHIP AT THE CUNARD PIER.

BELOW THOSE RESCUED FROM THE CLUTCHES OF THE OCEAN HUDDLE WITH BLANKETS AND HEAVY CLOTHES ABOARD *CARPATHIA*. THE PASSENGERS FROM THE RESCUING SHIP MADE EVERY EFFORT TO COMFORT AND AID THE SURVIVORS.

SAVED: THE STATISTICS

Just as there is no agreement as to how many people sailed on Titanic, *the estimates of survivors vary significantly. After a head-count, Captain Rostron indicated that 705 boarded* Carpathia. *The British Board of Inquiry, however, arrived at the figure 711, whilst White Star's official list, published a week after the tragedy, claimed 757 people lived through it. More recent studies have arrived at other figures, but it is widely accepted that the number saved was roughly 700 out of approximately 2,200 aboard – meaning that more than two-thirds of those on* Titanic *died.*

The Survivors

According to Captain Rostron, there were now 705 extra people aboard *Carpathia*: 705 individuals thankful to be alive, but 705 confused souls, mourning for lost family, friends and colleagues. Many were also physically injured, mentally exhausted and distressed about lost possessions. Their emotions were in a whirl, while for four hours Rostron made his way through the ice fields about which *Titanic* had been warned.

There were, of course, those who had, beyond hope, found loved ones they had thought lost. Ruth Dodge and her four-year-old son had been in Lifeboat 5, the second one sent out. It was not until her son said that he had seen his daddy aboard *Carpathia* but had been playing a game by hiding

from him, that she discovered her husband had reached safety in Lifeboat 13.

Equally fortunate was Nellie Becker, who was travelling with her three children. When Lifeboat 11 was loaded, four-year-old Marion and one-year-old Richard were placed in it, and it was declared full. Nellie screamed that she needed to be with her children, and she was allowed in, but her daughter Ruth, aged 12, was not. Ruth eventually went into Lifeboat 13, and, like the Dodges, was unexpectedly reunited with her family aboard *Carpathia*.

Leah Aks, a third-class passenger born in Poland and travelling to join her husband, had one of the more traumatic ordeals of those in the lifeboats. As she waited for Lifeboat 11, one of the stewards suddenly grabbed her 10-month-old baby, Frank, and literally tossed him into the boat. When Leah tried to retrieve him, she was restrained by other stewards, who thought she was attempting to push her way onto the

boat. Soon thereafter, the now-distraught woman was seated in Lifeboat 13, where Selena Rogers Cook and Ruth Becker tried to comfort her. Hours later, aboard *Carpathia*, Leah and Selena passed a woman holding a baby, whom Leah recognized as Frank, but the woman – supposedly either Elizabeth Nye or Argene del Carlo – claimed the baby as her own. Leah and Selena went to Captain Rostron, and after Leah described a birthmark on Frank's chest, he was returned to her.

Two children not so easily reunited with their parent were Michel and Edmond Navratil, aged three and two. As increasingly desperate people

BELOW AND BACKGROUND THE PASSENGERS ABOARD *CARPATHIA* DID THEIR BEST TO HELP THE SURVIVORS FROM *TITANIC*, BUT FOUND MANY OF THEM TOO SHOCKED BY THE EVENTS AND THEIR LOSSES TO BE ABLE TO BE COMFORTED.

LEFT A BADGE FOR A STEWARD FROM FIRST CLASS. ON ITS REVERSE SIDE IS ENGRAVED THE NAME "TOMMY", WHICH IS PRESUMABLY THE NAME OF THE STEWARD WHO WORE IT.

ABOVE MALE SURVIVORS OF THE *TITANIC* DISASTER ALL SHOW THE SAME HOPELESS LOOK. MANY OF THE MEN WHO SURVIVED WERE NEVER VIEWED OR TREATED THE SAME AGAIN.

THE TALE OF J BRUCE ISMAY

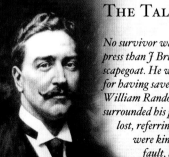

No survivor was treated more harshly by the American press than J Bruce Ismay, who became the tragedy's scapegoat. He was lambasted in editorials and cartoons for having saved himself when so many died, and William Randolph Hearst's New York American surrounded his photo with pictures of widows of those lost, referring to him as "J Brute Ismay". The British were kinder, the inquiry finding him free of any fault, and many praising him for helping load women into boats before his own departure. Nonetheless, he remained guilt-ridden for the rest of his life.

ABOVE The Navratil children: two-year-old Edmond (left) and Michel, aged three. The "*Titanic* orphans", known only as Lolo and Momon, stayed in New York with fellow passenger Margaret Hays until their mother arrived from France.

ATTACHMENT
A landing card issued to *Titanic* survivor Edwina Trout so that she could disembark from *Carpathia* and clear immigration in New York. Although British by birth, she remained in the United States after the tragedy, first in Massachusetts and later in California.

COFFINS AND CORPSES

Within hours of Titanic *sinking, White Star initiated an attempt to recover the bodies of those who died. On 17 April, the cable ship* Mackay-Bennett *left Halifax, Nova Scotia, with more than 100 coffins and several (tonnes) tons of ice for preserving. In a week-long search, 306 bodies were found: 116 so totally unrecognizable that they were buried at sea and 190 that were brought back to Halifax. In the following weeks three other ships found another 22 bodies. In total, 150 victims were buried in cemeteries in Halifax and 59 were claimed by relatives and buried elsewhere.*

had crushed around Collapsible D in the moments before it was launched, second-class passenger Michel Hoffman had passed the two children through the stewards to the boat. But Hoffman went down with *Titanic,* and after *Carpathia* arrived in New York, the story of the two orphans was carried in newspapers around the world. Only then did it transpire that Hoffman, whose real name was Navratil, had stolen his sons from their mother – from whom he was unhappily separated – hoping she would join them all in the United States. In May, White Star Line arranged Marcelle Navratil's passage to New York, and she was able to take her two boys back to France.

Another son who lost his father was 21-year-old R Norris Williams. When *Titanic* began to go down, he and his father tried to swim away from the ship. To his amazement, Williams came face to face with Gamon de Pycombe, the award-winning bulldog of first-class passenger Robert W Daniels, which was doing likewise. Williams' father died when a funnel collapsed on him, but the subsequent wave helped push the son towards Collapsible A, onto which he was pulled. On *Carpathia*, one of the doctors recommended amputating Williams' legs, which had been severely damaged by the cold water. Williams ignored the advice, and eventually was able to resume his tennis career.

Meanwhile, the hundreds aboard *Carpathia* were treated to thunderstorms, heavy rain and thick fog on the slow, woeful voyage to New York. There, on 18 April, before some 30,000 onlookers, Rostron eased his ship up to the Cunard pier, the first step for the former *Titanic* passengers in making a very different entrance to the New World than they had expected.

ABOVE The men of *Mackay-Bennett* had the most disheartening – and gruesome – job of all: finding bodies that told the terrible facts of the tragedy.

BOTTOM LEFT Third Officer Herbert Pittman (in the pale cap) speaks to Second Officer Charles Lightoller (with the pipe) just after their return to Liverpool aboard *Adriatic* on 11 May.

BOTTOM RIGHT When most of the surviving crew of *Titanic* arrived in Plymouth on 29 April, they were temporarily kept from rejoining their families or friends while they were interviewed one by one by Board of Trade officials.

COVERING AN INTERNATIONAL SENSATION

The loss of *Titanic* was one of the greatest news events of all time. Well before the survivors were even rescued, rumours about it had flashed over the wireless throughout the world. By the time Harold Cottam and Harold Bride began transmitting the list of survivors (information not immediately made available to the public), most newspaper editors had already made the assessment that any damage to the "unsinkable ship" would be an inconvenience rather than a tragedy. *The Daily Mirror* of London, for example, produced a headline stating "EVERYONE SAFE", while proclaiming "Helpless Giant Being Towed to Port by Allan Liner".

BACKGROUND In the days following the tragedy, crowds amassed outside the White Star Line office in Leadenhill Street, anxiously awaiting any news of *Titanic* and her survivors.

LEFT The front page of *The Daily Mirror* on 16 April 1912. After initially reporting that everyone was safe, it, like other papers, backtracked to acknowledge the disaster that had occurred.

RIGHT The coverage by *The New York Times* of the *Titanic* disaster is considered one of the masterpieces in the history of American journalism. The front page on 16 April shows how advanced its coverage was.

CARR VAN ANDA

The coverage of the Titanic *disaster was only one of many triumphs for Carr Van Anda, who is often considered the greatest managing editor in American journalistic history. Van Anda left Ohio University after only two years to become a journalist. He worked for progressively prestigious newspapers until, at age just 28, he became night editor of* The Sun *in New York. In 1904 he was hired by Adolph Ochs to rejuvenate the newsroom of* The New York Times, *and he subsequently built it into the finest news-gathering organization in the United States.*

BELOW For several days after *Titanic*'s demise, huge crowds constantly swarmed around the White Star Line offices in New York, London and Southampton hoping for news – which proved to be distressing more often than not.

One newspaper, however, did not make such assumptions. It was 1:20am on 15 April when a bulletin reporting that *Titanic* had struck an iceberg and was sinking at the bow reached the newsroom of *The New York Times*. Carr Van Anda, the managing editor, immediately made calls to correspondents

in Halifax, a wireless station in Montreal that had received the news via the steamer *Virginian*, and officials of the White Star Line. The last had not received an update since the first wireless report. Unlike other editors, Van Anda reasoned that the terrible silence meant only one thing: it had not been possible to send more messages. He immediately reorganized the first page of the late edition, with articles about the famous people aboard, previous times ships had collided with icebergs, other vessels that had reported ice in the region, and, in a bold box, the latest news as it had come through the wireless. When the paper went to press at 3:30am, not only did it give more background than any other newspaper, it was the only major daily newspaper to report flatly that *Titanic* had gone down.

By the next day, businessmen, families of those aboard *Titanic* and the curious public all crowded outside newspaper offices, Lloyd's at the Royal Exchange and White Star's headquarters in London, Southampton and New York, waiting for information. Many of the newspapers being sold on the streets still claimed that all the passengers had been saved. But the headline of *The New York Times* stated: "TITANIC SINKS FOUR HOURS AFTER HITTING ICEBERG; 866 RESCUED BY CARPATHIA, PROBABLY 1250 PERISH; ISMAY SAFE, MRS. ASTOR MAYBE, NOTED NAMES MISSING". By 17 April, the thorough coverage by Van Anda's team had led to newspapers around the world lifting material straight from *The New York Times*.

But Van Anda's greatest success was still to come. With *Carpathia* scheduled to arrive at 9:30pm on 18 April, this gave him only three hours to cover the biggest story in the world before the first edition went to press at 12:30am. He hired an entire floor of a hotel near Cunard's pier, fully staffed it with editors and installed four telephone lines directly to the rewrite desk of *The New York Times*. He also sent 16 reporters to cover every aspect of the story, although it had already been determined that no newspaper could have more than four passes to the pier and no one would be allowed on the ship until all survivors had left. The reporters and accompanying photographers were assigned in advance to almost every imaginable angle of the story.

ENCLOSURES
1 A letter to Sir Walter Howell of the Marine Department of the Board of Trade from Ismay, Imrie & Co. Dated 15 April, it indicates that it appears there is no danger of loss of life.
2 One of the first reports of the collision was this daily memo from Captain J J Knapp, the Hydrographer of the US Navy calmly reporting the collision of *Titanic* with an iceberg and noting previous reports of bergs or heavy ice.

INTERVIEWING HAROLD BRIDE

Van Anda's greatest coup was gaining an exclusive interview with Harold Bride. Wireless inventor Guglielmo Marconi planned to speak to Bride and Harold Cottam; Van Anda, who was Marconi's good friend, persuaded him to do it aboard Carpathia *and to take* The New York Times *reporter Jim Speers with him. Backed by a little bluster, Speers was able to board the ship with Marconi long before any other reporters. At Marconi's request, Bride gave Speers an extended account of the disaster. The next day it appeared verbatim over five columns of the front page, and it is still considered one of the most gripping stories in newspaper history.*

Van Anda's careful organization paid off. Friday morning's first edition contained 15 pages (out of 24) about *Titanic*, including an interview with Bride that was the journalistic highlight of the entire tragedy. Almost a century later that edition is still considered a masterpiece of newspaper history. More importantly, *The New York Times* coverage of the disaster helped greatly to secure the reputation and financial position of a newspaper that had been struggling, and to establish it as one of the world's key centres of journalistic innovation and excellence. Years later, when Van Anda was visiting the British press baron Lord Northcliffe, his host pulled a copy of *The New York Times* from 19 April 1912 out of his desk. "We keep this", he said, "as an example of the greatest accomplishment in news reporting".

The Official Inquiries

At 10:30am on 19 April, little more than 12 hours after *Carpathia* reached New York, a US Senate investigation into the disaster officially opened. It has been argued that it was convened to establish responsibility; to prove negligence, therefore providing American passengers with the right to sue *Titanic*'s owners; or to force the enactment of new maritime legislation. Regardless, it quickly became a personal forum for the inquiry's chairman, Michigan Senator William Alden Smith. In 17 days of testimony over five weeks, Smith used his position as chairman to dominate the questioning, despite showing a remarkable ignorance of ships and navigation.

The first of 82 witnesses was J Bruce Ismay, who was interrogated about the ship's speed, the damage incurred from the ice and how he obtained a place in a lifeboat. Other witnesses included the four surviving officers, wireless operator Harold Bride, wireless inventor Guglielmo Marconi, 34 crew members and 21 passengers. Captain Stanley Lord and two men from the ship *Californian* were also questioned; they told of a mysterious ship that fired a number of rockets before, after failing to respond to signals, simply disappearing. Significantly, Smith did not interview a single officer who had been on the bridge of *Californian* on the night of 14/15 April.

By the end of the hearings, testimony and affidavits filled 1,145 pages. In his report, Senator Smith rebuked the British Board of Trade for not requiring enough lifeboats, criticized Captain Smith for his lack of precautions in an area of ice, praised Captain Rostron and denounced Captain Lord for failing to aid *Titanic*. Smith concluded that *Californian* was far closer to *Titanic* than the 30.5 kilometres (19 miles) reported by Lord, saw her distress signals and failed to come to her rescue, initiating a controversy that continues today. Smith also made several significant recommendations: that it become mandatory for ships to carry lifeboats with a total capacity to hold each person aboard; that lifeboat drills be instituted for crew and passengers and that wireless equipment be manned 24 hours per day.

Before the American investigation was even finished, the British Board of Trade initiated its own Court of Inquiry, with 72-year-old Lord Mersey serving as commissioner, and Attorney General Sir Rufus Isaacs as counsel to the Board of Trade. Officially, there were 26 topics – including issues of construction, *Titanic*'s speed, ice warnings received, number of lifeboats and behaviour of the crew and passengers – for which the inquiry was attempting to gain information and find answers. But although there were ultimately 96 witnesses =and 25,622 questions and answers – many believe that from the start, Mersey had an agenda: to whitewash any negligence by the Board of Trade and the White Star Line, and to find a culprit to whom he could attach blame.

The inquiry was wide-ranging in those questioned, from the crew to Marconi to Antarctic

The Ordeal of Sir Cosmo Duff Gordon

Perhaps the most publicized sideshow of the British inquiry was the testimony of Sir Cosmo Duff Gordon. He was questioned extensively about his offer of £5 to each of the crew aboard Lifeboat 1, which was viewed by many as a bribe so they would not return to rescue those in the water. Clearly none of the interrogating barristers believed him when he denied hearing any suggestions about going back. Lady Duff Gordon's subsequent testimony did not help her husband's credibility, and although Sir Cosmo received no official censure, his public reputation was ruined.

explorer Sir Ernest Shackleton, but it generally followed the issues raised in the American inquiry. Under the circumstances, Mersey's conclusions were totally predictable. Both Ismay and Sir Cosmo Duff Gordon were exonerated. No blame was found in the treatment of third-class passengers. Although it was ruled *Titanic* was going too fast, Captain Smith was cleared of negligence. Both the Board of Trade, which had let *Titanic* sail without the necessary lifeboats, and the White Star Line were absolved of any significant fault, meaning that their financial liability was limited.

But there was still a need for a scapegoat and, having long had his mind made up in this regard, Lord Mersey easily found one. He held that *Californian* had been the "mystery ship", as close as eight kilometres (five miles) away, and that she could have easily reached *Titanic* but had not made the effort. Thus, it was not the lack of lifeboats, excessive speed or even the iceberg responsible for the tragedy; it was the officers of *Californian*, and most notably, Captain Lord.

LIGHTOLLER ON THE STAND

One of the most impressive performances during the inquiries was by Second Officer Charles Lightoller. Questions posed in both countries tried to show that the White Star Line – via its captain and senior officers – had been negligent, and should therefore be liable for damages. However, Lightoller proved extremely able at protecting White Star and avoiding any admission harmful to his former colleagues. He emphasized the unusual weather conditions and claimed that no ship's captain reduced speed under such a situation. His testimony helped both White Star and Captain Smith to escape without significant blame.

ABOVE SIR ERNEST SHACKLETON, A FORMER OFFICER FOR THE UNION-CASTLE LINE, WHO HAD GAINED WORLDWIDE FAME AS AN ANTARCTIC EXPLORER, TESTIFIED TO THE BRITISH INQUIRY ABOUT NAVIGATING SHIPS IN ICE-COVERED WATERS.

TOP SIR COSMO DUFF GORDON RECEIVED INTENSIVE – AND RATHER CONFRONTATIONAL – INTERROGATION DURING THE BRITISH BOARD OF TRADE INQUIRY, PARTICULARLY FROM W D HARBINSON, THE COUNSEL FOR THE STEERAGE PASSENGERS.

ENCLOSURE
Part of a set of correspondence responding to a call by President Taft for ideas on how the great loss of life in shipping tragedies could be prevented in the future. Many letters stated the obvious: proceed more slowly and carefully in areas of ice and pair ships so there would always be a rescue vessel. Those responses with technological innovations range from simplistic and even silly to extensively considered, designed in great detail and already patented.

RIGHT GUGLIELMO MARCONI, THE INVENTOR OF THE WIRELESS AND THE 1909 NOBEL PRIZE WINNER IN PHYSICS, TESTIFIED AT BOTH INQUIRIES REGARDING THE USE OF THE WIRELESS FOR SAFETY AND GENERAL COMMUNICATIONS AT SEA.

CALIFORNIAN AND THE MYSTERY SHIP

For decades, Captain Stanley Lord of *Californian* has been cast as the villain of the *Titanic* disaster for failing to respond to her distress signals. Ever since the official inquiries determined that the two ships were closer to each other than Lord stated, many have assumed that *Titanic*'s "mystery ship" was *Californian*. But putting aside the desire to find a culprit, what do the facts actually indicate?

A cargo vessel of 6,223 tons, *Californian* left Liverpool for Boston on 5 April. On the night of 14 April, surrounded by loose ice, *Californian* stopped at a position calculated as 42°05'North, 50°07'West, 35 kilometres (22 miles) north of the remains of *Titanic*. At about 11pm, Lord saw the lights of what he considered a small steamer, and asked wireless operator Cyril Evans which other ships were nearby. Evans only knew of *Titanic*, but the ship Lord saw was far too small for that. Nevertheless, Lord ordered Evans to contact *Titanic* about the ice; he was promptly cut off by Jack Phillips.

By 11:30pm, the ship's green starboard light was visible about eight kilometres (five miles) away, but Third Officer Charles Groves was unable to make contact by Morse lamp. When Second Officer Herbert Stone replaced Groves on watch at midnight, he ordered apprentice James Gibson to continue Morsing the ship. Then, at 12:40am, a series of rockets began to shoot through the mysterious ship's rigging. In the next hour, eight rockets appeared, which puzzled Stone, because the ship began to steam away, which was unexpected from a ship in distress. At about 2:20am she disappeared. Stone sent Gibson to inform the captain, who was sleeping, but Lord later stated that, perhaps because he was exhausted, he could not remember being given such information.

Around 5:00am, going onto deck, Lord saw a ship about 13 kilometres (eight miles) away. He ordered Evans to contact her, and when the operator turned on the wireless, he heard about *Titanic*. Lord immediately headed to the coordinates that had been transmitted from the doomed ship, where he found the steamer *Mount Temple*, but nothing else. Continuing on, he met *Carpathia* and continued the search for survivors.

Lord testified in the US hearings, but found that sensational newspaper reports of statements by crewman Ernest Gill had already influenced Senator Smith. Smith's negative position was bolstered by Captain John Knapp of the US Navy, who created a map showing positions he attributed to *Titanic* and *Californian* and "proving" they were seen by each

RIGHT CAPTAIN STANLEY LORD, SHOWN LEAVING THE SCOTTISH DRILL HALL WHERE THE BRITISH INQUIRY WAS HELD, WAS UNFAIRLY MADE THE SCAPEGOAT BY BOTH INQUIRIES, RUINING HIS CAREER.

BELOW THE SS *MOUNT TEMPLE*. WHEN *CALIFORNIAN* ARRIVED AT THE COORDINATES JACK PHILLIPS HAD BROADCAST, ALL THEY FOUND WAS *MOUNT TEMPLE* UNDER CAPTAIN JAMES HENRY MOORE.

BACKGROUND LEFT AN ACCOUNT BY HENRIK NAESS OF HIS TIME ABOARD *SAMSON*, IN WHICH HE CLAIMS THOSE ABOARD SAW THE ROCKETS LAUNCHED BY *TITANIC*.

THE TREACHERY OF ERNEST GILL

Ernest Gill was a crewman who deserted after Californian *arrived in Boston. For almost two years' wages, he sold to the press a sensational and clearly fabricated story about a vessel he could see in distress at the time the rockets were fired. Because of this tale, Gill was one of three men from* Californian *to appear before the US Senate inquiry, where his testimony was inconsistent and at odds with other accounts and reports. Nevertheless, it allowed Smith's search for a scapegoat to focus upon Captain Lord, who paid the price for Gill's avaricious scheme.*

other. These positions were highly inaccurate, but helped produce Smith's condemnation of Lord.

The British inquiry followed the Senate's lead, despite numerous major discrepancies, including that the sound of *Titanic*'s rockets would have been audible to any vessel in sight, that both *Titanic* and *Californian* were stationary but the mystery ship was moving, and that a ship the size of *Titanic* would be unmistakable at close range. Lord Mersey chose to ignore any data or testimony in favour of his pre-determined scapegoat, and, as Lord was called only as a witness, with no charges against him, he was unable to defend himself. Lord's reputation was ruined, and he was soon forced to resign from the Leyland Line. Despite later efforts, he died in 1962 without clearing his name.

The discovery of *Titanic* in 1985 in a location significantly different than that Phillips transmitted was further proof that *Californian* was not the mystery ship, and that she could not have reached *Titanic* in time to save the passengers even if Lord had steamed towards the disaster area immediately after the rockets had been seen. Seven years later, the first official vindication of Lord was produced, when a Department of Transport investigation determined that *Californian* was 27–32 kilometres (17–20 miles) away and out of sight of the sinking liner. The final report indicated that the officers of *Californian* had indeed seen the rockets of *Titanic* through the rigging, but that any fault in failing to act lay with Second Officer Stone.

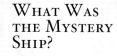

BELOW Crew of Californian summoned to give evidence at the British inquiry. Among those pictured are wireless operator Cyril Evans, apprentice James Gibson and Second Officer Herbert Stone (third, fourth and fifth from left).

ABOVE RIGHT In later years, *Samson* was purchased for Admiral Richard Byrd's Antarctic expedition, during which she was known by the new name of *City of New York*.

What Was the Mystery Ship?

The abundant proof that Californian was not the mystery ship does not indicate what actually was. In the most authoritative study on the subject, Titanic *expert Senan Molony gave many options, while also demonstrating that, given the distance between ships, there was possibly more than one – meaning that the ship seen from* Titanic *might not have been the same as that seen from* Californian. *Although numerous vessels have been suggested as the mystery ship, one strong candidate is the Norwegian sealer* Samson. *In 1962, a 50-year-old report by her first officer was found, which indicated that she was operating illegally; the captain, worried that the rockets were from a government fisheries vessel, simply sailed away.*

ENCLOSURE
A letter from Captain Stanley Lord defending himself from the findings of Lord Mersey. Also shown in background.

BACKGROUND TOP LEFT The original statement of Second Officer Herbert Stone of *Californian* about the night of 14/15 April.

After the Tragedy

It was 1913, and "Craganour", owned by Charles Bower Ismay, had just won the Derby at Epsom. The signal "Winner All Right" had been given so that payments on bets could be made, and the horse had been taken to the Winner's Circle. Suddenly the stewards, despite no official complaint having been registered, announced that "Craganour" had jostled several other horses and that they had awarded the victory to "Aboyeur". Was the rumour true – that the racing establishment would never let a horse owned by an Ismay win the Derby? No one really knows, but the story adds a twist to one definite fact: that the sinking of *Titanic* not only changed forever the lives of many who survived the tragedy, but also of others only tangentially involved, such as J Bruce Ismay's younger brother.

Despite the lack of censure by the British board of inquiry, Ismay himself was never to escape public disapproval for living when so many others died. The same was true of Cosmo Duff Gordon, who lived with allegations about his lack of bravery until his death in 1931, six years before Ismay. Sadly, the same blame attached to other men who had survived, including Major Arthur Peuchen, Dickinson Bishop (who was the subject of unfounded rumours of having entered a boat dressed as a woman) and the ship's officers, none of whom ever gained promotion to captain in the merchant fleet.

Conversely, the events gained fame for some of the players in the tragedy. Arthur Rostron was awarded the Congressional Medal of Honor and the American Cross of Honor and went on to command *Caronia*, *Lusitania* and *Mauretania*. He was knighted in 1926. Margaret "Molly" Brown's heroism and care for others aboard *Titanic*, in Lifeboat 6 and on *Carpathia*, made her a national figure, and she was immortalized in the Broadway musical, later to become a feature film, *The Unsinkable Molly Brown*.

The Titanic Graveyards

After the remains of 59 victims of the disaster were claimed, 150 bodies remained in Halifax. Their burials began on 3 May, and many people attended to honour those being interred so far from home. The Titanic plot at Mount Olivet Cemetery was intended for Catholics, and 19 individuals were buried there. The plot at Baron De Hirsch Cemetery, which received ten bodies, was intended for Jewish victims, but some were buried elsewhere, and Michel Navratil was mistakenly interred there because he had used the alias Hoffman. The other 121 victims, initially presumed to be Protestants, were placed in Fairview Lawn Cemetery.

hymn-sing on the evening of the collision, was met by her fiancé in New York, where the two were married that week. They moved to a farm in Oregon, where they lived together for 49 years. Dr Washington Dodge survived with his wife and son, but suffered a mental breakdown in 1919 and committed suicide. Second-class passenger Edwina Trout suffered emotional problems for months, but recovered and eventually moved to California. There she outlived three successive husbands and became a popular figure at *Titanic* events, dying in 1984 at the age of 100.

Eleanor Widener, Emily Ryerson and Madeleine Astor all later remarried, Madeleine thus relinquishing all claim to the Astor fortune. Their previous families were not forgotten, however. In August 1912, Madeleine gave birth to a son, whom she named John Jacob Astor V. The body of her late husband had been one of the most easily identifiable of those found by *Mackay-Bennett*, his initials discovered in his shirt collar and his effects including a gold watch, gold and diamond cufflinks, a diamond ring and $2,440 cash. Eleanor Widener commemorated her son lost on *Titanic* with a $3.5 million donation to build the Harry Elkins Widener Memorial Library, the primary building of the Harvard University library system.

Although some survivors found it easy to rebuild their lives, others did not. Charlotte Cardeza, who had occupied the most expensive cabin on the ship, seemed most concerned about replacing the 14 trunks, four suitcases and three crates of baggage she and her son had brought aboard. She filed the largest claim against the White Star Line, seeking $177,352.75 for her losses. Marion Wright, who had sung a solo at the second-class

Finally, two of the key ships in the *Titanic* story suffered similar fates. During the First World War, in November 1915, *Californian* was torpedoed by an enemy submarine in the Mediterranean. She sank, but only one man was lost. In July 1918, *Carpathia* was crossing from Liverpool to Boston when she was also torpedoed – three times. She took two and a half hours to sink, and all but five of the 280 aboard were rescued.

LEFT JOHN JACOB ASTOR IV, WHO WAS ONE OF THE MOST PROMINENT, AND THE RICHEST, OF THOSE LOST IN THE TRAGEDY.

ABOVE AND BACKGROUND THE BODY OF A VICTIM IS RECOVERED FROM THE OCEAN. SO MANY BODIES WERE RECOVERED THAT THE CABLE-SHIP *MACKAY-BENNETT* WAS NICKNAMED THE "FUNERAL SHIP".

BELOW *OLYMPIC*, THE SISTER SHIP OF *TITANIC*. OF THE THREE GREAT SHIPS ENVISIONED IN 1907 BY J BRUCE ISMAY AND LORD PIRRIE, SHE WAS THE ONLY ONE TO LEAD A FULL LIFE, FINALLY BEING RETIRED IN 1935.

WHAT HAPPENED TO *OLYMPIC* AND *BRITANNIC*?

Titanic *was not the only one of White Star's three giant ships to meet an early demise. The third was originally to be named* Gigantic *but was launched in 1914 as* Britannic. *Serving as a hospital ship in the First World War, she either struck a mine or was torpedoed in 1916 in the Aegean, and sank within an hour.* Olympic, *on the other hand, had a long career after being given a refit to increase her lifeboat capacity, raise her bulkheads and build a new inner skin. She spent much of the Great War as a naval transport ship, but then returned to regular service, making hundreds of Atlantic crossings before being retired in 1935, after which she was stripped of her fittings and scrapped.*

Search and Discovery

The dream of finding, or even raising, *Titanic* is virtually as old as the tragedy itself. Shortly after the disaster, several wealthy families – the Astors, Guggenheims and Wideners – proposed that the Merritt and Chapman Derrick and Wrecking Company conduct a salvage operation for the ship, but the technical limitations of the time simply did not allow such a venture to go ahead. In the following half-century, a succession of schemes was proposed, most of them totally impractical.

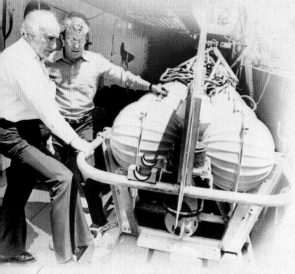

In 1980, the first serious attempt to locate the ship was launched. Flamboyant Texas oil millionaire Jack Grimm and film producer Mike Harris led an expedition on the research vessel *H J W Fay* to find *Titanic* using side-scan sonar. Grimm's party searched a broad area in the vicinity where Jack Phillips had reported *Titanic* to be. But like Grimm's earlier well-publicized searches for the Loch Ness Monster, Big Foot and Noah's Ark, this one was unsuccessful. Grimm and Harris returned to the area in 1981 and again in 1983, but bad weather and sea conditions (and not looking in the correct place) meant they found nothing.

Success was finally achieved, not by publicity- or treasure-hunters, but by marine geologist Robert Ballard of the prestigious Woods Hole Oceanographic Institution in Massachusetts.

Ballard had dreamed of locating *Titanic* as far back as 1973, not only for the knowledge that could be gained, but as a means of testing new developments in underwater photography. By the mid-1980s, he was the head of Woods Hole's Deep Submergence Laboratory, and his group had developed an underwater video camera vehicle named *Argo* and was working on a small, remote-controlled deep-sea robot called *Jason*. Intrigued by the possibilities of this equipment, the US Office of Naval Research agreed to fund a three-week test of *Argo*, which would be used in a search for *Titanic*.

In 1985, Ballard's team and researchers from the Institut français de recherche pour l'exploitation des la mer (IFREMER, or The French Research Institute for Exploitation of the Sea) under Jean-Louis Michel joined together. They began with a month aboard the French research vessel *Le Suroit*, using a new French side-scanning sonar system to make detailed sweeps over a 240-square-kilometre (150-square-mile) area to the south and east of *Titanic*'s last stated position. The criss-cross pattern they followed became known aboard ship as "mowing the lawn". They covered approximately 80 per cent of the designated area, but found nothing before having to leave to attend to other scientific projects.

Much of the team then transferred to the Woods Hole research vessel *Knorr*. The operation continued, using the sonar and underwater video cameras aboard *Argo*. For two weeks *Argo* was hauled back and forth, but nothing was found, even when the search area was extended farther east. But early in the morning of 1 September, the watch monitoring the images from *Argo* began to see man-made

RIGHT The men who found *Titanic*. From left: Jean Jarry, the French project leader; Robert Ballard of Woods Hole and Jean-Louis Michel, who co-led the expedition at sea with Ballard.

LEFT Jack Grimm (left) with Bill Ryan of Lamont-Doherty Geological Observatory, Columbia University, aboard *Gyre* in 1981. They are shown with a magnetometer, a sensing device to be used on the ocean floor.

BELOW It was not all fun and games in the search for *Titanic*, as shown by these members of the crew of *Le Suroit* launching a deep-sea sonar in rough waters.

The *Argo* System

The discovery of Titanic *was the culmination of Ballard's development of a remotely controlled, deep-sea visual-imaging system. Designed by Stu Harris of Woods Hole's Deep Submergence Laboratory, by 1985* Argo *had a steel frame some 4.5 metres (15 feet) long, one metre (3.5 feet) wide, one metre high and weighing 1.8 tonnes (two tons). It was equipped with a series of lights, several components to determine its positioning and three video cameras recording at different scales and covering different angles, the images from which were instantly relayed to a control centre on the ship.*

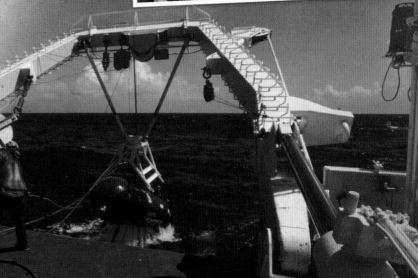

LEFT A SIGN THAT WAS CREATED ABOARD *Knorr* IN HONOUR OF HER SUCCESSFUL SEARCH FOR *TITANIC* IN 1985. IT WAS SIGNED BY BOTH THE AMERICAN AND FRENCH MEMBERS OF THE EXPEDITION.

LEFT THE WOODS HOLE OCEANOGRAPHIC INSTITUTION RESEARCH VESSEL *KNORR*. THE REMOTELY CONTROLLED VEHICLE *HERCULES* – A SUCCESSOR TO *ARGO* – IS BEING BROUGHT ABOARD AFTER A DIVE OFF SICILY IN 2003.

RIGHT AND BACKGROUND THIS SMALL COLLECTION FROM THE THOUSANDS OF DISHES ABOARD *TITANIC* TELLS A BIT OF THE TRAGIC TALE OF HOW EVEN THE STRONGEST AND RICHEST EFFORTS OF MAN CANNOT OVERCOME NATURE.

BELOW ONE OF THE BOILERS THAT SITS IN THE DEBRIS FIELD BETWEEN THE TWO SECTIONS OF *TITANIC*. IT IS LIKELY THAT SOME OF THE BOILERS PLUNGED TO THE BOTTOM BEFORE THE SHIP FINALLY BROKE ASUNDER.

the sunken ship, knowing that if the cable to the surface snagged on any of *Titanic*'s features the invaluable piece of equipment could be lost forever. On their final day, Ballard sent down *Angus*, an unmanned sled with an array of still cameras, and it snapped thousands of pictures of the bow, the debris field and, at the far end of the debris, 600 metres (1,970 feet) away, what careful analysis would later show to be the stern.

Ballard and company then turned regretfully towards Woods Hole, not yet realizing that this was only the first step in the new existence of *Titanic*.

wreckage, and then a vast boiler appeared. There could be no doubt about it – they had found *Titanic*.

In the following two days, a storm blew in, with winds gusting up to 40 knots and waves of 4 metres (14 feet) smashing against *Knorr*. But *Argo* continued to transmit pictures from 4 kilometres (2.5 miles) below, and at the end of the long debris field the investigators found the bow of the ship, sitting upright on the ocean floor. With time running out before *Knorr* had to go to another scientific project, they guided *Argo*'s passes over

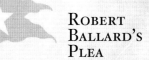

ROBERT BALLARD'S PLEA

At the press conference following the discovery of Titanic, *Ballard expressed his hopes that the historic ship be treated with dignity and respect, rather than being plundered. "The* Titanic *itself lies in 13,000 feet [4,000 metres] of water on a gently sloping, alpine-like countryside overlooking a small canyon below," he said. "There is no light at this great depth and little light can be found. It is quiet and peaceful and a fitting place for the remains of this greatest of sea tragedies to rest. May it forever remain that way and may God bless these found souls."*

LEFT THE RETURN OF *KNORR* TO WOODS HOLE ON 9 SEPTEMBER 1985 WAS MET BY A GROUP OF WELL-WISHERS AND REPORTERS. THE RELATIVELY SMALL CROWD WAS A SLOW BEGINNING TO THE MEDIA FRENZY THAT WOULD FOLLOW.

The Exploration of Titanic

ABOVE AN UNDERWATER RESEARCH ROBOT USED BY IFREMER DURING THE INCREASINGLY COMPETITIVE INVESTIGATION OF *TITANIC*.

Robert Ballard now knew exactly where *Titanic* was located, and in 1986 he led another expedition, this time to explore the great wreck. His efforts were again primarily funded by the Office of Naval Research, with an official goal of testing *Jason Junior* (or *JJ*), the prototype of the Deep Submergence Laboratory's remote-controlled underwater robot with photographic capabilities. Meanwhile, the French withdrew from the project after the initial images of *Titanic* were released by Woods Hole before IFREMER received them.

In July, Ballard's party was taken to the *Titanic* site aboard *Atlantis II*. Over a period of 12 days they made ten dives in *Alvin*, a research submersible modified to sustain the pressure of great depths and to house *JJ* on its bow. Each dive took up to ten hours, including two and a half to descend some 4,000 metres (13,000 feet) and the same to return to the surface.

The first dive had to be severely curtailed owing to a salt-water leak into the battery pack that powered *Alvin*. Ballard and two colleagues had just enough time to locate *Titanic*'s bow, which suddenly loomed through the darkness in front of them like a monstrous wall of black steel rising straight from the seabed. It was the first time human beings had seen *Titanic* itself in almost three-quarters of a century. They then ascended to avert the potential technical disaster in the sub, but the sight had been enough to drive the programme full-speed ahead in the ensuing days.

The problems with *Alvin* were soon resolved, and on the second dive Ballard and his team landed on *Titanic*'s mighty forward deck to find, much to their amazement, that the wood planking was gone; only the metal sub-deck survived. They soon realized that undersea worms and wood-boring molluscs had consumed most of the ship's wood, although some of the harder varieties, such as teak, remained in the interiors. Other softer materials

The Fate of Titanic's Bow

Ballard's investigation answered many questions about how Titanic *broke up. As the sinking bow forced the stern higher out of the water, the ship finally snapped between the third and fourth funnels, a structural weak point because of its large open spaces, such as an engine room air-shaft and the aft Grand Staircase. The bow followed the angle in which it already pointed, and planed down, gathering speed until it reached the seabed, and burying its nose 18 metres (60 feet) into the sediment. The rest of the bow bent as it settled onto the bottom, and as it did so, the decks near the tear in the hull collapsed upon themselves.*

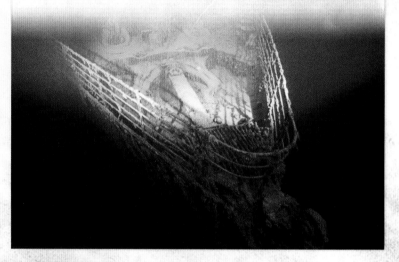

ABOVE AND BACKGROUND THE BOW SECTION OF *TITANIC*. IT SMASHED INTO THE SEABED WITH SUCH FORCE THAT IT WAS BURIED 18 METRES (60 FEET), UP TO THE STARBOARD ANCHOR. ALTHOUGH THE AREAS OF THE FORECASTLE NEAR THE CAPSTANS AND ANCHOR CHAINS SEEM LITTLE DAMAGED, THE FOREMAST HAS COLLAPSED BACK UPON THE BRIDGE, WITH THE CROW'S NEST STILL ATTACHED TO IT. THE AREAS FARTHER BACK HAVE COLLAPSED IN UPON THEMSELVES FROM THE IMPACT OF SMASHING INTO THE OCEAN BOTTOM.

LEFT *JJ* EXPLORING THE STARBOARD FORECASTLE DECK. LIT UP IN THE LITTLE ROBOT'S LIGHTS IS A BOLLARD COVERED BY SEVEN DECADES' WORTH OF RUST AND DAMAGE CAUSED BY IRON-EATING BACTERIA.

– including paper, cloth and human remains – had also disappeared through the ravages of time and deep-sea organisms. Ballard also investigated the opening above where the fore Grand Staircase had stood and the collapsed area at the rear of the bow section.

In the following days, Ballard made an intensive examination of the two major sections of the wreck and the debris field between and around them. Key to the success of the operation was Martin Bowen's control of *JJ*. He dropped the small robot, known by some as the "swimming eyeball", down the Grand Staircase as far as B deck, and also sent it to explore areas too small or confined for *Alvin* to enter. Meanwhile, *Alvin* and *JJ* between them took thousands of photographs.

The mangled stern was the most distressing area to investigate because they knew so many people had died there, having moved progressively farther back as the bow went under the water. Although it was sitting upright and facing the same direction as the bow, it was a picture of carnage: exploded, fragmented and jumbled. As with the bow, Ballard hoped to be able to learn from it more about the actual injury caused by the iceberg. But like the bow, it was buried too deeply to allow an exact

determination of the extent of any damage.

Between the two major portions of *Titanic* was a field of debris almost 610 metres (2,000 feet) long. There were thousands upon thousands of items littering the bottom, including lumps of coal; metal objects such as heaters, pots and pans, wrought-iron benches, bedsprings and the ship's safes; and all manner of non-metallic materials, such as bathtubs, floor tiles, bottles, statues from public rooms, plates and cups and numerous passenger effects.

When *Atlantis II* ran out of time, Ballard and company turned back towards the US. It had been a sobering experience, but Ballard was pleased to think that, because of the condition *Titanic* was in, it was at least impossible to salvage her. However, there were others who had entirely different thoughts.

ABOVE Divers work to raise items taken from the debris field in the vicinity of the two large sections of *Titanic* to the surface. Thousands of items have now been collected from the deep waters.

LEFT The remains of a deck bench – the wood attached to it long since consumed by undersea creatures – was discovered in the debris field near the wreck of *Titanic*.

RIGHT The stern section of *Titanic*. The stern appears more damaged than the bow, because it dropped more or less straight down instead of planning. It then hit the seabed with such violence that it was buried 14 metres (45 feet) at points, and caused the decks near the tear in the ship to collapse down onto one another.

THE SINKING OF THE STERN

The stern of Titanic *did not sink as quickly as the bow, which had already filled with water. But as it descended, the force of the water rushing in pushed out the air, the violence ripping open the poop deck and thrusting it backwards onto itself. Dropping more or less straight down, it slammed into the seabed so hard that it was buried to about 14 metres (45 feet) at the rudder. The force of hitting the bottom caused the decks to collapse onto one another and the outside plating to crumple and bulge outwards.*

THE SALVAGE OF TITANIC

Once Robert Ballard's team discovered *Titanic*'s location, it was apparent that the wreck would prove an irresistible draw for those wishing to study it, photograph it or retrieve artefacts. The following year, Titanic Ventures, of Connecticut, USA, teamed up with Ballard's former French partner, the IFREMER to conduct scientific studies, make photographic records and engage in recovery operations on *Titanic*. Over two months, 23 dives were made from IFREMER's ship *Nadir* in the submersible *Nautile*, during which some 1,800 artefacts were taken from the debris field and the wreck itself. Unfortunately, it has been argued that the care normally shown at significant archaeological sites was not taken, and some damage to *Titanic* occurred – such as when the crow's nest bell was pulled from the mast, in the process of which the crow's nest itself collapsed.

The retrieval of items from the ship caused enormous controversy, and efforts were made in the US Congress to prevent such operations, but, as *Titanic* lies in international waters, such efforts came to nothing. Many of the objects gathered in 1987 were put on display in a series of exhibitions around Europe, but the promise of the organizations involved to treat the artefacts with dignity was called into question when some of them appeared in *Return to the Titanic ... Live*, a sensationalized French television show inexplicably hosted by American actor Telly Savalas, who showed little knowledge of *Titanic*.

In 1991, a joint Russian–Canadian expedition spent three weeks filming *Titanic* for what eventually became the IMAX movie *Titanica*. The next year, a new company, Marex-Titanic, Inc., set off on a salvage operation, but Titanic Ventures went to court to stop the effort, launching several

WHAT SURVIVORS SAID

Like the general public, Titanic *survivors who were still alive when the salvage began had a wide range of views about the operations. Eva Hart was one of the most outspoken critics. "The ship is its own memorial. Leave it there," she said, adding that it was her father's grave, and "you don't go poking around in someone's grave". But Beatrice Sandström wrote that, "I am personally pleased ... Your presentation of the recovered objects from the ship will help to teach the present and future generations the timeless human lessons learned from this great marine tragedy."*

years of legal wrangling. In 1993, RMS Titanic, Inc. acquired the assets and liabilities of Titanic Ventures, and thereupon launched a new expedition in conjunction with IFREMER. Making 15 dives, they brought back some 800 artefacts, including a set of the ship's whistles and one of the lifeboat davits.

Some of the items collected in 1993 were introduced into a court with maritime jurisdiction in Virginia, and the following year a US district court declared RMS Titanic, Inc. the salvor-in-possession of the wreck and entire *Titanic* site. This ruling excluded anyone else from visiting the site to gather artefacts, and has limited operations of others to filming or viewing the ship and location.

Since that ruling, RMS Titanic, Inc. has conducted another five expeditions, the first three in conjunction with IFREMER. In 1994, 700 more artefacts were gathered, as well as more than 170 pieces of coal, some of which have since been sold. Two years later, efforts were made to answer some of the questions about the disaster by taking an international team of biologists, naval architects, historians and metallurgists to examine the wreck and conduct a broad range of investigations into the remains. RMS Titanic, Inc. also conducted expeditions in 1998, 2000 and 2004.

BELOW Allan Carlin, general counsel for RMS Titanic Inc with the "Big Piece", the largest section of Titanic that has actually been able to be brought to the surface and then to land.

THE BIG PIECE

Knowing that it was impossible to raise the bow or stern of Titanic, *in 1996 RMS Titanic, Inc. focused on a separate, 17-ton section of the hull nicknamed the "Big Piece". The Big Piece was raised to 61 metres (200 feet) below the surface by means of diesel-filled flotation bags, and the expedition ship* Nadir *attempted to haul it to New York. Two days later, the cables holding the Big Piece failed, and it resank. In 1998, it was raised again, this time to the surface, and attached to the ship* Abeille Supporter. *It has been exhibited in the US and extensively treated for preservation.*

ABOVE The key to the binocular store for the *Titanic's* crow's nest. Second Officer David Blair accidentally left with it when he was transferred off the ship in Southampton. Despite it being unlikely that any binoculars were in the storage compartment anyway, the key sold for 130,000 euros at an auction in 2007.

After the early controversy, the salvage issue became less objectionable to much of the public after the National Maritime Museum in Greenwich, England, agreed to stage an exhibition of artefacts. Entitled "The Wreck of the *Titanic*", it opened in October 1994 with a ceremonial ribbon-cutting involving two survivors, Mrs Edith Brown Haisman and Miss Millvina Dean. The exhibition proved so popular that it was extended for six months and was viewed by approximately 750,000 people.

Despite the success of the exhibitions at the National Maritime Museum and other museums around the world, there remain many who still feel it inappropriate to gather artefacts from what they believe to be a gravesite. The managers of RMS Titanic, Inc. insist that the operation will protect, conserve and restore the recovered artefacts, in the process helping the public learn about and understand *Titanic* and her place in history. As with so many other debates or questions about *Titanic*, this argument is likely to rumble on.

BELOW One of the deckchairs from *Titanic*. Because the chairs floated, some of them were more easily salvaged by men from the early ships visiting the location of *Titanic's* demise.

ABOVE After several years of preparatory efforts in 1998 the "Big Piece", a 15-tonne (17-ton) section of *Titanic's* hull, was brought to Boston. It has since been exhibited and considerable conservation and research has been carried out.

BACKGROUND A life jacket from *Titanic*. It is uncertain how many such relics still exist, but their value has increased incredibly in recent years. Purchased a decade ago for under a dollar, this one was recently valued at $25,000.

BELOW Millvina Dean opens a *Titanic* exhibition in Southampton. Only two months old when she was saved with her mother and brother, she is now believed to be the last living survivor of *Titanic*.

TITANIC REMEMBERED

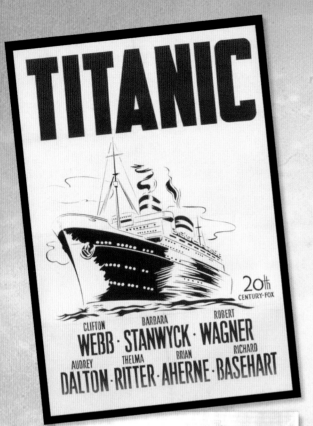

TITANIC IN THE MOVIES

Many films, whether on television or the big screen, have featured Titanic *in a cameo role or have drawn part of the plot from her story. The movies that actually derive from and emphasize the tale of the tragedy include:*

1912	Saved From the Titanic
1912	In Nacht und Eis
1943	Titanic
1953	Titanic
1956	A Night to Remember *(television)*
1958	A Night to Remember
1964	The Unsinkable Molly Brown
1979	S.O.S. Titanic
1980	Raise the Titanic
1995	Titanica
1996	Titanic *(television)*
1997	Titanic
2003	Ghosts of the Abyss

No other shipwreck in history has made such an indelible imprint upon the imagination as that of *Titanic*. The events of the tragedy never truly left the consciousness of the Western public, but the excitement generated by Robert Ballard's discovery of *Titanic*'s resting place, and then the huge success of James Cameron's blockbuster film of 1997, have made certain that the tale will continue to fascinate people throughout the world.

Just as happens today, immediately after the tragedy several books were hastily produced to capitalize on public interest. A more thoughtful and serious work was *The Truth About the Titanic*, written by historian Archibald Gracie, a first-class passenger who corresponded with other survivors to collect a broad range of information and opinion. But sadly, he did not live to see its popular reception, dying in December 1912 aged only 53, having never fully recovered from swimming to the overturned Collapsible B and staying atop it all night in wet, freezing clothes.

At the same time, second-class passenger Lawrence Beesley, who had escaped on Lifeboat 13, produced *The Loss of the SS* Titanic: *Its Story and Its Lessons*, which has long been considered one of the most insightful, informative and reasoned accounts. Since the works by Gracie and Beesley, more than 850 books about the disaster have appeared, as well as innumerable articles.

More than a dozen films have also told parts of the story, the first starring and co-written by 22-year-old silent movie star Dorothy Gibson, who had survived in Lifeboat 7. Released on 14 May 1912, less than a month after *Titanic* sank, it was given outstanding reviews by film trade magazines, but was widely criticized elsewhere for being insensitive to those who had lost loved ones. Such lack of feeling was nothing, however, when compared to a version three decades later made under the auspices of Nazi propaganda minister Joseph Goebbels, and showing the true hero to be a German passenger. What is frequently considered the best film of the tragedy was *A Night to Remember*, which appeared in 1958 based on a book of the same name, and starred Kenneth More as Second Officer Charles Lightoller and David McCallum as wireless operator Harold Bride. But none of these could match the financial

RIGHT A POSTER ADVERTISING THE 1958 FILM *A NIGHT TO REMEMBER*, WHICH IS STILL WIDELY CONSIDERED THE BEST FILM EVER MADE ABOUT THE TRAGEDY.

TOP AN ADVERTISING POSTER FOR ONE OF SEVERAL FILMS NAMED *TITANIC*, THIS ONE STARRING CLIFTON WEBB, BARBARA STANWYCK AND ROBERT WAGNER.

RIGHT A SCENE SHOWING THE LOADING OF LIFEBOATS IN *A NIGHT TO REMEMBER*, STARRING KENNETH MORE AS CHARLES LIGHTOLLER.

ABOVE A POSTER ADVERTISING JAMES CAMERON'S *TITANIC* AS A LOVE STORY ABOARD THE SHIP.

FAR RIGHT LEONARDO DECAPRIO AND KATE WINSLET ARE CONFRONTED WITH THE FLOODING OF THE AREA AROUND THE FIRST-CLASS STAIRCASE IN JAMES CAMERON'S *TITANIC*.

RIGHT JAMES CAMERON, WHO WAS THE DRIVING FORCE BEHIND THE 1997 BLOCKBUSTER *TITANIC*.

BACKGROUND A POSTER FOR THE 1980 ADVENTURE FILM *RAISE THE TITANIC*.

success of Cameron's version with Kate Winslet and Leonardo DiCaprio. In the following years, Cameron followed up by making numerous dives to the remains of the ship, culminating in the IMAX film *Ghosts of the Abyss*, which featured extensive footage of the wreck.

Cameron's film initiated the largest wave yet of interest in *Titanic*. Memorabilia of all forms has been produced in recent years and, along with original posters, photos, books and other items, has made *Titanic* a booming business. No aspect of this is more widespread than postal stamps produced throughout the world. Enthusiasts have been able to purchase stamps featuring *Titanic* (although many include inaccurate representations of the ship or events) from countries as diverse as Angola, the Bahamas, Barbados, Eire (The Republic of Ireland), Gambia, Grenada, Guyana, Kyrgystan, Liberia, Madagascar, the Maldives, Mali, Niger, Romania, Russia, Sierra Leone, St Vincent and the Grenadines, the United Kingdom, the United States and the former Yugoslavia.

Similarly, there are societies and clubs around the world dedicated to *Titanic*. The foremost is

RIGHT THE *TITANIC* MUSEUM IN INDIAN ORCHARD, MASSACHUSETTS HOLDS A HOST OF EXCITING ARTEFACTS FROM THE DOOMED SHIP.

BELOW RIGHT *TITANIC: THE MUSICAL* OPENED IN APRIL 1997 TO GREAT SCEPTICISM FROM THE CRITICS.

the *Titanic* Historical Society, founded in 1963 by Edward S Kamuda, and maintaining the Titanic Museum in Indian Orchard, Massachusetts. The society has thousands of members drawn from all over the world, many conducting research into the ship, her passengers and her tragic voyage. The museum features such items as the ship's original blueprints from Harland & Wolff, Frederick Fleet's discharge book and the life-jacket worn by Madeleine Astor.

Keeping up with technology, there are also innumerable websites devoted to *Titanic*, a selection of which is found in the Further Reading section (see page 63). Through all of these efforts, the memories of *Titanic* and the disaster that befell her are preserved.

ATTACHMENT
A letter on behalf of the daughter of J Bruce Ismay and the son of Stanley Lord stating that the film *A Night to Remember* inaccurately portrayed their fathers and requesting that every showing of it be preceded and followed by a statement referring to the letter's protest.

TITANIC: THE MUSICAL

The tragedy of Titanic *is not something that one might normally consider appropriate to sing about, but the difficulties facing such a proposition were overcome in 1997 when* Titanic: The Musical *opened on Broadway. Although plagued early on with technical problems and criticized for its story-line before it even opened, the musical became a huge success and ran at the Lunt-Fontanne Theatre for 804 performances. Despite taking great liberties with the facts (including who lived and died), it broke box office records for 15 consecutive weeks before winning five Tony Awards, including Best Musical.*

The Enduring Legacy

The individual bravery and heroism shown by those who died on *Titanic* caught the spirit of the age in the final years before the Great War, a time when sacrifice for God, country, mankind's progress or a noble ideal was still most honourable – and honoured. Before long, many memorials – statues, plaques, church windows, fountains, even entire buildings or structures – were dedicated to those individuals and groups of people who lost their lives when *Titanic* went down.

Nowhere were the dead more universally mourned than in Britain, and in no city more so than Southampton, the home of a large percentage of the crew. There, in 1914, a magnificent tribute to *Titanic*'s engineers was dedicated in East Park. A different Southampton memorial honoured the ship's postal workers, another the musicians and yet another the stewards, sailors and firemen. Liverpool, the official home of the White Star Line, also built multiple memorials, and numerous towns created cenotaphs by which to remember their native sons, including orchestra leader Wallace Hartley in Colne, Lancashire, shipbuilder Thomas Andrews in Comber, County Down, Northern Ireland and, across the Atlantic, Major Archibald Butt in Augusta, Georgia. The most extravagant building prompted by the disaster is the Harry Elkins Widener Memorial Library at Harvard, financed by Eleanor Widener in memory of her son.

Despite the many poignant monuments and the numerous books, films and other ways of remembering the tragedy and the individuals who died in it, the greatest legacy of *Titanic* was the worldwide legislation it prompted to establish safer sea travel. Both the American and British inquiries demanded that new safety regulations be put in place, and soon thereafter ships were required to carry enough lifeboats to hold everyone aboard, to conduct lifeboat drills and, for those with 50 or more people, to have a 24-hour radio watch. The public reaction to the tragedy also forced the governments most heavily involved in Atlantic shipping to take action; not long after the disaster, shipping lanes were shifted south, away from the ice. In addition, international meetings relating to safety at sea were scheduled.

Meanwhile, the US Navy assigned two cruisers to patrol the Northwest Atlantic in the general

region of the Grand Banks, where *Titanic* had sunk, and keep shipping informed of ice. The next year, the Navy was unable to perform this function, so it was taken over by the US Revenue Cutter Service, the forerunner of the US Coast Guard. This safety measure proved so successful that when the first International Conference on the Safety of Life at Sea was convened in London in late 1913, the major maritime nations joined to create the International Ice Patrol (IIP). The

International Convention for Safety of Life at Sea

One of the major triumphs of the London conference in 1913 was the agreement on the International Convention for Safety of Life at Sea (SOLAS), which came into force the next year. An updated second version was adopted in 1929, a third in 1940, a fourth in 1960 and the current one in 1974. SOLAS has wide-ranging provisions, specifying minimum standards for the construction, equipment and operation of ships. Numerous amendments have been made to SOLAS 1974, in order to keep abreast of technological developments and make ships as safe as possible.

functions assigned to the IIP were to patrol the Northwest Atlantic during the season of iceberg danger, monitor and track icebergs in that region, provide information to shipping about the limits of known ice and attempt to keep the transatlantic lanes clear.

Following the experience gained in 1912 and 1913, this task was turned over to the US Coast Guard, with expenses initially shared among the 13 nations most heavily involved in transatlantic navigation. In recent years, the governments contributing to the operation have included Belgium, Canada, Denmark, Finland, France, Germany, Greece, Italy, Japan, the Netherlands, Norway, Panama, Poland, Spain, Sweden, the United Kingdom and the US.

The US Coast Guard has continued to operate the IIP for nine decades, with the exception of the years during the two world wars. Today, the IIP makes regular surveillance flights from Hercules HC-130 aircraft and combines the information obtained with that from all ships operating in or passing through the ice area. Data relating to icebergs, ocean currents and winds allow for the twice-daily projection of iceberg locations and ice limits over the radio and internet. As a result, since the inception of the IIP, no loss of life or property has occurred because of a collision with an iceberg in the area monitored.

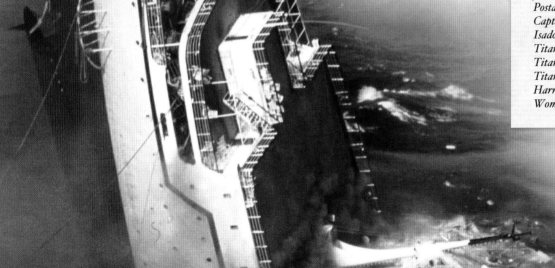

LEFT SADLY, DESPITE SAFETY REGULATIONS, DISASTERS STILL OCCUR. IN AUGUST 1991, THE GREEK CRUISE LINER *OCEANOS* SANK OFF THE SOUTH AFRICAN COAST WHILE SAILING BETWEEN EAST LONDON AND DURBAN. LIKE *TITANIC*, SHE SEEMED TO STAND ON END BEFORE SINKING, AND AS WITH THE OLDER SHIP, NOT MUCH WAS LEFT BEHIND OTHER THAN DECKCHAIRS.

BELOW AND BACKGROUND A FLORAL ARRANGEMENT FROM THE INSTITUTE OF MARINE ENGINEERING SCIENCE AND TECHNOLOGY – IN THE SHAPE OF A WHITE STAR LINE FLAG – IS LAID AT THE MEMORIAL DEDICATED TO *TITANIC*'S ENGINEERS, WHICH WAS OPENED AT A CEREMONY IN SOUTHAMPTON'S EAST PARK IN APRIL 1914.

ABOVE A HERCULES HC-130H AIRCRAFT, SPECIALLY BUILT FOR THE US COAST GUARD WITH TWO SCANNER STATIONS, ADDITIONAL CREW POSTS AND A VARIETY OF OTHER FEATURES FOR THE INTERNATIONAL ICE PATROL.

TITANIC MEMORIALS

There are many memorials in 21 different countries to the individuals or groups of people lost aboard Titanic. *Among the most notable are:*

Thomas Andrews Memorial Hall: Comber, County Down, Northern Ireland, UK
Major Archibald Butt Memorial Bridge: Augusta, Georgia, USA
Father Thomas Byles Memorial Window: St Helen's Church, Ongar, Essex, England, UK
Crew, Stewards, Sailors and Firemen Memorial Fountain: Southampton, England, UK
Engineers Memorial: Liverpool, England, UK
Engineers Memorial: Southampton, England, UK
Wallace Hartley Memorial: Colne, Lancashire, England, UK
William Murdoch Memorial: Dalbeattie, Dumfries & Galloway, Scotland, UK
Musicians Memorial: Liverpool, England, UK
Musicians Memorial: Southampton, England, UK
John Phillips Memorial Cloister: Godalming, Surrey, England, UK
Postal Workers Memorial: Southampton, England, UK
Captain Edward Smith Memorial: Lichfield, Staffordshire, England, UK
Isador and Ida Straus Memorial Fountain: New York, USA
Titanic Memorial: Belfast, Northern Ireland, UK
Titanic Memorial: Cobh, Eire (Republic of Ireland)
Titanic Memorial Lighthouse: New York, USA
Harry Elkins Widener Memorial Library: Cambridge, Massachusetts, USA
Women's Titanic Memorial: Washington DC, USA

RIGHT A CONTEMPORARY PIECE OF ART COMMEMORATING THE LOSS OF *TITANIC*. THIS ONE, WHICH EMPHASIZES THE BRITISH AND AMERICAN PASSENGERS AND CREW, IS MADE OF WOVEN SILK.

INDEX

Page numbers in *italic* refer to picture captions